Mender
of the
BROKEN

by
Willie Kerry

PALADIN
PUBLISHING

Mender of the Broken
ISBN: 978-1-7360332-0-3
Copyright © 2021 by Willie Kerry

Published by Paladin Publishing
P. O. Box 700515
Tulsa, OK 74170

Scriptures are taken from the following sources:
The Holy Bible, New International Version®, NIV®, copyright © 1973, 1978, 1984, International Bible Society.
The Message (MSG), copyright © 1993, 1994,1995, 1996, 2000, 2001, 2002 by Eugene H. Peterson. Used by permission of NavPress Publishing Group.
The Holy Bible, New Living Translation, copyright © 1996, 2004. Used by permission of Tyndale House Publishers, Inc., Carol Stream, Illinois 60188. All rights reserved.
The Holy Bible, English Standard Version, ESV®. Text Edition: 2016. Copyright © 2001 by Crossway Bibles, a publishing ministry of Good News Publishers.
The *King James Version (KJV)* of the Bible.

Text Design: Lisa Simpson

Note: Names and some details have been changed to protect the privacy of individuals.

Printed in the United States. All rights reserved under International Copyright Law. Contents and/or cover may not be reproduced in whole or in part in any form without the express written consent of the Publisher. No part of this publication may be reproduced, stored in a retrieval system, or transmitted in any form or by any means—electronic, mechanical, photocopy, recording, scanning or other—except for brief quotations in critical reviews or articles without the prior written permission of the Publisher.

ENDORSEMENTS

Abuse, struggles, forgiveness, freedom. In spite of a life in continual darkness, "Willie" was eventually able to find a life of Truth in Jesus. She found God's Light at every turn and the sweetness of His grace each time she felt she could not go on. You will read from beginning to end in one sitting. You will experience every emotion with regard to Willie. You will feel sorry for her, be angry with her, and rejoice with her. Please read Willie's story—a reminder that we can come back from anything with God's help.

Gail Marten,
Author of *It's All About Balance*

Riveting. Against the backdrop of immeasurable pain and darkness, the light of Jesus does its most powerful work. What a compelling story of hope, freedom, and restoration.

Kelly Wood, Co-pastor
The Assembly, Tulsa, OK

I absolutely loved this book! My heart ached for Willie, but the work of the Lord is so evident in her heart and life. This letter was inspiring. and the words of redemption give such hope to so many who are hurting. I believe this letter will be used to help others.

Rebecca, RN
Tulsa, OK

Mender of the Broken is for anyone whose pain, however incurred, led them down a deep, dark path. The writing depicts a heart-wrenching story of abuse, abandonment, and betrayal and the poor choices it produced. Yet, the author doesn't leave you there but demonstrates the unfailing and unrelenting love of a Heavenly Father who, even when everything looks hopeless, can make all things new.

Brett M. Hutton
Author and Pastor

Truly authentic and raw, the author lets you in on the details of her life and the places she has been, physically, emotionally, and spiritually. Coming from someone with similar pain from the past, I could relate as she vulnerably revealed the highs and low of a broken life and the desperate need for wholeness. The inspiration and encouragement the author provides comes from a healed heart of experience through tragedy. This letter pleads to be read by anyone that has gone through or is going through a life of sadness and regret. The answer to a turn-around is found within these words.

Chelsi Zwart-Singleton
Leader of Propel – The Assembly (Tulsa, OK)

DEDICATION

There are so many precious saints who loved, supported, and encouraged me while I shared my life and heart with you. Too many to name, but I know their hearts. They would want all the recognition and glory to go to Jesus.

So, I dedicate this book to God. To my Father, to my Savior and friend Jesus, and to the Holy Spirit. If it were not for their divine intervention, I would not be alive today.

But God had a purpose and a plan for my life.[1] I say, "Thank You, Jesus, for breaking down every barrier that kept me from receiving Your love. Thank You for shattering the chains that kept me in bondage for years."

Contents

Introduction 9
Chapter 1 My Letter to You 19
Chapter 2 Lights Out 25
Chapter 3 Ann and Jean 31
Chapter 4 Wrong Place at the Wrong Time 35
Chapter 5 The Farm 41
Chapter 6 Did Anyone Miss Me? 49
Chapter 7 The Shame Game 53
Chapter 8 Revelation Dream 57
Chapter 9 North County Mental "Hell"
  Institution 63
Chapter 10 There's No Place Like Home 79
Chapter 11 Angels Unaware 91
Chapter 12 More Angelic Assistance 113
Chapter 13 Choices and Consequences 145
Chapter 14 Moving Forward 173
Chapter 15 Nothing Between Us 183
Chapter 16 The Power of the Tongue 189
Endnotes 197
Resources 201
A Note from the Author 205

Introduction

I began writing this letter in 2013, but it all began, as best as I can remember, in 1968. Divulging my deepest, darkest secrets is risky. But I know someone needs what is written in these pages. Someone out there is yearning to be loved, heard, and validated. Others are feeling trapped and abandoned. Some are so brokenhearted they cannot fathom the idea of embracing a loving Savior.

The sting of abuse is often too hard to face, so we live in denial and pretend as though nothing ever happened. Those of us who have lived in that deep darkness know that we can never completely escape those memories or the damage the abuse caused. But God **can and will** do exceedingly abundantly more than we could ask or even imagine.[2] He heals our hearts and minds. He changes our will to desire His. He mends our souls. The Spirit of God is doing this for me, and He will do it for you! Allow yourself to cry out to Jesus as I finally did. I promise you, He is near! He will hear you and respond in ways you never expected or ever dreamed possible!

I say, "He is doing it" because the process is always ongoing. It requires daily surrender. We need to believe we are who Jesus says we are—not who we have been convinced we are. He loves us so much, and if we are His, He has redeemed us. And we must live in a way that reflects that. This can sometimes be a daunting commission. But we have His Holy Spirit to help us and guide us every single day!

Had the Lord not intervened in my life, I would have ended up in prison, working the streets to survive, or even dead. I was on the verge of surrendering to total darkness. But He reached down, offered me His nail-scarred hand, and pulled me out of the muck and mire that was my life. His offer of redemption was only one grasp away, but for a long time I was afraid to accept it. I did not have a single bone in my body that trusted anyone.

But I did know how broken my heart was, how broken my life was, and how desperately I wanted to feel worthy of something, to be able to point to something good or virtuous in myself. So, although I was terrified, I finally reached back, and something amazing happened. God assured me He would make everything from those horrendous years work together for my good. How He was going to accomplish that, I didn't know. But I began to imagine a life free from fear, self-judgment and doubt.

Introduction

I still have scars, and although they will always be part of me, I now understand their purpose.

Behind each scar was a divine intent—that my deliverance from a life of guilt and shame would be a testimony to the deep, abiding love of Christ. Our scars tell us where we have been, but they DO NOT govern our future.

I am still tempted to think some things are better left hidden. I am talking about choices I have made in life that have left a trail of destruction. I had almost convinced myself that sharing them would not help anyone and would only make deep, intimate relationships impossible. But I could no longer ignore the prompting of the Holy Spirit. I knew I had to give myself permission to be vulnerable and let these parts of my life speak hope into someone else's heart.

Our life experiences can bring healing and hope to others. It is my prayer that this account of my life, this personal letter to you, will do just that. It is raw and painful, but it shows the reality of walking in sin and darkness. But it also reveals an even greater, more wondrous story of Divine Love.

The events of my early childhood could have destroyed me as I matured into adulthood, except God had a different plan. Grace consumed the dark forces that surrounded my life! Up until the time I made the decision to trust and follow Jesus, I had no idea that Christ had already won the war for my soul.

In 1982, a dear Christian woman introduced me to Jesus. Her name was Cathy. This was my intervention moment. I had no idea the Holy Spirit was about to do a work in my heart and open my eyes and my ears to the truth of the Gospel. The Lord showed up in an amazing way. Being the "All Knowing" God that He is, He knew the depth of my doubt and insecurity and knew what it would take for me to believe.

Cathy ran the day care where my two children spent much of their time. She was a kind and gentle woman. She was also a Christian. At the time I didn't exactly know what that meant; I only knew she lived her life completely dependent on her God. That was clear. She radiated peace every day. Nothing provoked or disturbed her. I watched her as she spoke to her God about everything. She was in constant fellowship with Him. I thought she was a little crazy at first, always talking to the air. But the way she responded to those conversations caused me to pause and pay attention. Cathy would always tell me that God was Love. Every chance she got, she would speak God's truth into my life, even though at first, I was opposed to hearing what she had

INTRODUCTION

to say. She knew about all the disgrace, shame, and self-doubt I carried heavy in my heart. Although I denied it had any affect on my life, I knew that was a lie, one I would prefer to take to my grave. Even though I claimed those humiliations as my lot in life, she spoke only what God the Father said about me. I wanted to press my hands over my ears and tell her to stop talking because I felt those assurances did not apply to me. Besides, a Heavenly Father did not appeal to me at all! My experience with a father was anything but love and goodness. But Cathy was determined to obey the voice of God no matter how I responded. She knew that He was after my soul. I was His child and she knew it.

This was why the Lord chose her to watch my children. Cathy was relentless in her determination to make me hear. How grateful I am now that she didn't give up on me. When I finally began to listen, the power of God's Word became unmistakably real.

She told me how treasured I was to God. She said He was a loving Father and that He created me to love and to be loved no matter what my earthy father had done to me.

She began to share the words of Scripture to me. "I am the Creator and you are My creation. I breathed into your nostrils the breath of life."[3] "I knit you together in your mother's womb."[4] "I know the number of hairs on your head, and before a word is on your tongue, I know it."[5] "You are fearfully and wonderfully made."[6]

She told me that if I would just believe God, if I would accept His free gift of salvation, He promised to make me a brand-new creation. Flashes of my past raced through my heart, and I couldn't imagine there was enough mercy to keep it from blinding me. She saw I was struggling but continued to read.

The old has passed away; the new has come.[7] You've been saved by grace.[8] You've been justified by faith.[9] You are utterly secure in Me; nothing will be able to separate you from My love in Christ Jesus.[10] No one is able to snatch you out of My hand.[11]

Even after hearing the truth from God's Word, I still had a hard time believing God was talking about me. I knew the depth of my sin. Nevertheless, something in my heart longed to believe that every horrible choice I had made and disgusting act I had participated in were washed away. Cathy asked me to pray with her and I said yes!

It didn't happen instantly while I sat there with Cathy listening to her pray for me and with me. It was entirely too intimate for my comfort. But when I got home that night, put the kids to bed, and waited for Donny to go to work, God did a miracle in my longing for love in my heart. I sat down in the quiet of my small little home and began to read the parts of the Gospel of John Cathy had highlighted for me. It was there my eyes were opened, and the truth of God's Word pierced my heart. Cleansing tears came streaming down my face until my heart overflowed.

It's important to remember that the words spoken over us and the ones we speak over ourselves have power. Words have the power to heal or destroy. Life and death are in the power of the tongue![12] I spoke Life into my life, because I **believed** the Word.

Even after I put my faith in Jesus Christ, I still struggled with believing the truth about how Christ saw me and how deeply He loved me. Many new believers struggle with this, and it is okay. God knows and He will bring us through it! He made a promise to me, and I knew it was true. He said, **"I will never leave you nor forsake you."**[13] This promise has been evident in my life since that glorious day in June of 1982 until today. God has been faithful to continue the work He began in my heart and mind that day, and I have no doubt He will complete it. He never breaks a promise!

Scripture tells us: "Therefore, there is now no condemnation for those who are in Christ Jesus."[14] It also says, "The truth will set you free."[15] Jesus **is** Truth, and knowing Him and accepting His free gift of grace sets us free from the law of sin and death. Once we embrace this freedom, we can begin to understand who we are and what our purpose is. Only then can we experience genuine peace and joy and be all we were created to be.

I pray this letter will shed divine light on what the cross truly represents and what the shed blood of Jesus has accomplished for us. His resurrection from the grave frees us fully and eternally from the consequences of our sin. Past, present, and future.

He took upon Himself all our sin, guilt, and shame. All of it! There is nothing we have done or ever could do that will separate us from the love of Jesus. If we believe in Him, we are washed clean, whether we feel clean or not.

Before reading any further, please stop and ask Jesus to open your heart to His love. Let Him speak His affection and grace into your life too.

NOTE: This is my story, and my process. There are quite a few people that were hurt by and are still struggling with what happened during what I refer to as the

Introduction

"Charles years." Likewise, the same is true for any other situation mentioned. Everyone experiences people and situations in their own way. Everyone's relationship is their own. I'm simply writing my process. I don't assume or expect anyone to see or feel things the same way I do as everyone has their own process and journey to walk through.

My Letter to You

But you are the ones chosen by God, chosen for the high calling of priestly work, chosen to be a holy people, God's instruments to do his work and speak out for him, to tell others of the night-and-day difference he made for you—from nothing to something, from rejected to accepted.[16]

efore we begin let's pray this together: Holy Spirit, please help us all to see clearly the purpose for our suffering, even if it is simply to identify with Your suffering. We all have a story that speaks of brokenness in one way or another. But it's in our brokenness that our self-will is shattered. It's the beginning of a life absolutely surrendered to Your will. Brokenness is often the road to breakthrough. I pray we have breakthrough now.

(Note: If you didn't read the introduction, please do so. It is necessary to understand what you will read next.)

Dear friend,

My name is Willie. It's an unusual name for a girl, but my fine Irish parents thought they were getting a boy when I made my grand entrance into this world. I sure surprised them. I guess they thought it's as good a name as any other, so it stuck.

I suppose the best place to start is the beginning—at least as far back as I can remember. I must be honest with you. There are a lot of gaps in my memory. Some are small segments of time and others are fairly long. I attribute this to a merciful God, who sovereignly and sympathetically hid certain memories to protect an already damaged heart. Isn't that just like our Heavenly Father?

If you don't know Him yet, I pray with all my heart that you will by the end of this letter.

I grew up in a home that was functionally dysfunctional. We all lived in a perpetual state of denial. Those on the outside saw a large but typical American family. But our family hid dark secrets. No one wanted to admit it, but there was an abusive spirit living in the Kerry home. Because reputation seemed to be everything to my parents, the potential repercussion of coming forward and tainting their status in the community or in the Catholic parish of St. Margaret's kept me in a continual state of fear. At least in the beginning.

We had a big family—four boys and three girls. I think my folks tried to do what they thought was best for our family. But that wasn't always true, especially when my dad was under the influence of alcohol. When he was in that state, even my mom was fearful of crossing him. She didn't protect us from him, and that is my only grievance toward my mom. The rest of her poor choices where I was concerned were simply due to a lack of understanding.

When alcohol got the best of my dad, which was often, I always seemed to be in the wrong place at the wrong time. Either that or I was handpicked by my dad to be the unlucky recipient of all his rage. That is certainly how it felt to me. The unleashing of his fury is what I remember the most. Those terrible times had lasting effects on my young mind and heart.

My parents were a very social pair, so our home wasn't completely devoid of laughter. It just wasn't the kind of amusement I felt safe or welcome around. It often involved liquor, and I knew I had better be seen and not heard. That decree was virtually written in stone.

Our family did travel from time to time, usually in our motor home. I always loved the family's favorite camping spot down in the Ozarks where we went quite often. I also have fond memories of our much anticipated yearly trips to Colorado, to visit another large Catholic family with almost as many kids. While my mom and dad stayed preoccupied with their adult friends, we kids were free to roam the lower mountain ranges of Colorado Springs. To this day, the smell of pine trees evokes some wonderful memories of a more playful time.

When each evening rolled around, and I knew it was time to make our way back home, I would begin to feel extremely fretful. I knew my dad would have been drinking most of the day, and if I wasn't vigilant to stay very alert and at a safe distance, I would find myself in trouble. What if I spoke before being spoken to? What if I was told to do something I knew I was incapable of doing? If I didn't obey, there would be hell to pay, but I was powerless to save myself from the situation. There was never a compromise with Dad or an opportunity to present a defense.

I believed that in some warped way, all of Dad's "rules" were simply "setups" for my failure. He seemed to know I would fall short of his unreachable standards. I figured that he needed a person to punish, since something demonic plagued his own soul.

In Dad's mind, even the smallest offense was construed as willful disobedience. Otherwise there would have been no justification for his cruelty. With my dad, disobedience was intolerable. When you combine even the perception of an insubordinate child with too many mixed drinks, the environment is ripe for a severe misuse of authority. His weapon of choice was the belt. It was like a sick game that nobody else seemed to be playing except my dad and me. And because he made up the rules as he went, I could never catch a break.

One day I saw my dad punch my little brother so hard it put him through the drywall of our house. The brutality was inconceivable. I felt so guilty because I was relieved that it wasn't me that time. I ran and hid, holding my breath for what seemed like an eternity and trying my hardest to get the image of my brother's terrified face out of my mind. As horrible as that scene was, nothing prepared me for what was to come.

After one terrifying night, I knew I could not face another morning.

I was ten.

Lights Out

I don't remember where everyone else was. I seemed to be alone in the house. I knew both parents were at work, and I was thankful for the brief reprieve. I was sinking in a swamp of sadness and grief.

I also knew that 5:00 p.m. would roll around soon enough, and I thought the next time I refused to comply with one of his demands my dad might actually kill me. Three nights before, he had proved he was capable.

Something happened. Something I did or said. I don't even remember what it was. Something had made my dad so incensed that I found myself locked in a downstairs bathroom, bent over the bathtub. I knew he was fully committed to using that infamous belt to exorcise whatever demon he thought possessed me. He beat me more ferociously than I had ever been beaten before. I screamed and pleaded for him to stop. I could hear my mom and sisters outside the locked door shouting at him to open it. They pounded on the door, and for a split second I thought they might break right through that lock. But my salvation never came. Instead, the flogging continued until I could no longer hear anything but the heaving of my dad's breath and the pounding of my own heart.

Just before going unconscious, I remember looking up at my dad and seeing the sweat dripping down his face. I saw eyes that were bloodshot and bulging. His lip quivered like a mad dog, and his teeth looked as sharp as razors. In that moment, at the very young age of ten—when most little girls are playing with dolls and having tea parties with their daddies—I was looking into the face of a devil. The beating continued. I blacked out.

A few days after being almost belted to death, all I could think about was how to escape all the pain. Physically, I was welted and bruised, and I hurt all over my body. Emotionally, I was shattered, and I couldn't bear another whipping. I didn't know the definition of or even the word "despair," but I knew I was plummeting deeper into some black abyss and I couldn't get out.

I had been taught during my catechism days at St. Margaret's that taking your own life was an unforgivable sin. I thought God would surely make an exception this one time. Though I'm not even sure I gave that more than a brief thought, because I needed the pain in my heart to stop, and I needed it to stop right away.

I went to my mom's medicine cabinet and emptied into my small hand pills from several bottles marked "take for pain." My soul was aching. I think I had at least six or eight pills securely detained in my hand. I held them like I felt, tightly trapped in my own grief. I know that one read valium; another was codeine of some kind. I also grabbed bottles whose label read, "For sleep." I went back to my bathroom and sat on the sink, looking at myself in the mirror. I remember saying to a sad and hollow-looking reflection, "Willie, you are going to die today." I started to cry.

I was scared, but something inside me would not let it overwhelm me. At least not yet. My experience three days prior overrode any doubt that going to sleep and never waking up would be a deliverance I would truly welcome. The tears quickly dried up, and I swallowed all of the pills at once.

I sat there for several minutes, watching and waiting for some sign that my demise was imminent. Suddenly

I was afraid to die. I needed to get to the phone and call my mom. She needed to know what I had done so she could rush home and save me. I needed her to assign such significance to my young life that she would call for my rescuers immediately.

As I wept over the phone and began to feel the effects of the pills I had ingested, I felt terrified. I will never forget the unsympathetic and merciless response I received from the other end. My mother laughed and said, "Oh, Willie, you will be fine. Just go sleep it off. Now I need to get back to work." And she hung up. No sirens, no rescuers, no tenderness. Just panic and an overwhelming sense of knowing I was broken and could not be fixed. That was when it happened.

The torture I endured in that locked bathroom, the many whippings prior, and the cruelty of my own mother's indifference changed something in my heart. All of it led to many years marked by darkness and destruction.

By this time, I saw life as pointless. I no longer cared what happened to me. It was my goal (conscious or not) to stay as anesthetized as I could and remain emotionally detached. If insubordination was what my dad hated the most, insubordination would be what he got!

As for my mom, I kept her at arm's length until my early twenties. All that mistrust and hurt meant we missed out on that special mother-daughter love and friendship.

All I wanted was to escape from my deep depression. But I couldn't overthrow this formidable foe, and it almost made me go insane. (I think on a few occasions I did.)

I wanted desperately to love and be loved, but all my attempts at trying to belong and fit in were overshadowed by the fact that no loving act on my part was ever reciprocated. And that filled me with hatred. The powers of the unseen world were waiting for me to unleash the wrath boiling inside me. Their goal was to fuel this spark of hatred in my heart into a full-blown blaze. Oh, the destruction that would ensue!

My four brothers were too young to understand the demons that permeated our home, and my two older sisters were afraid of the seditious nature of their baby sister. My sister Jean, who was only eleven months older, bore the brunt of my hostility, mainly because I had nowhere else to direct all the anger, and Jean was never shy in making sure I understood her aversion to me. I didn't feel like family, but like an outcast who was tormented by a bully every day on the playground—except my playground was my home, and the bully happened to be my own sister.

I ended up becoming one of the most rebellious adolescent girls this Irish Catholic family had ever seen. The bitterness in my heart would manifest itself in some very dangerous ways.

Something was churning inside my soul that was becoming more and more disturbing, and I knew that if there were not some sort of intervention soon, this time Jean would be in the wrong place at the wrong time. Soon she would be.

Ann and Jean

Ann was the oldest girl in our family, and Jean was daughter number two. I was the third girl, and we had four younger brothers. I don't fault Ann or Jean for how strained our relationships were. I was anxious and unsettled most of the time, and it made life very difficult for them—really for everyone. We struggled to develop a real bond, and I feel the effects, even to this day. But I love them both, and I know they love me. Family is family, even if I don't feel like part of it. And no matter what, we do our best to support one another. At least that is the Kerry motto. But it still makes me very sad that I don't have much of a rapport with my sisters. I often wish every member of my family had known God enough to cry out to Him, asking Him to restore us to wholeness. Repentance and forgiveness could have led to such healing.

I am not sure why my relationship with Jean was the most difficult. Maybe because we weren't even a year apart. Or because it was harder for her to tolerate my attitude. There was so much strife, tension, and even revulsion on both sides. At the time, I justified my horrible feelings toward her by maintaining she never had my back. I always found it suspicious that whenever Jean would become aware I had violated our dad's rules, he would inevitably find out. I never completely understood why she would do this, because Jean knew what the consequence would be. I was already hurting in ways that were beyond my ability to comprehend, let alone articulate. I just have to believe that she didn't know what else to do to bring order into her world. Maybe there were times she didn't rejoice at the harsh treatment I received on a regular basis—especially after she witnessed that horrible scene in the bathroom. If she ever felt sympathy for me, I am grateful. Maybe one day we can talk about it.

Although I don't think Jean ever got the infamous switch for a single act of impropriety, she still witnessed the secret madness in our home. Each one of us had our own set of coping skills. Jean just wanted all the

Ann and Jean

pandemonium to cease, and she saw me as the culprit for all the turmoil occurring at home.

Jean had secured allegiance from our parents by bringing home great grades, practicing pristine behavior, and agreeing to be the "Willie police." In my frustration, that is the title I gave her. Although I knew about many of her missteps, I never ratted on her.

Who would have believed me anyway? Maybe the priest at St. Margaret's. I was in the confessional a lot, and it was his duty to believe what his parishioners said. He would quickly redirect my confession to be about my own sins, not Jean's. I was secretly hoping my tattling on Jean would somehow get back to my dad, since I knew he and our priest shared what looked like to me a chalice of bourbon on occasion. Sadly, all the "Hail Mary's" and "Our Father's" he required never seemed to fix me. Neither did saying the Rosary on my knees.

I remember saying under my breath, "I don't think you have a cure for what I've got, Father." A sure indication that my "hope" meter was reading empty.

My oldest sister, Ann, was also a model daughter, only she really did come by it genuinely. But her head was buried so deep in the sands of denial that an earthquake could not have jarred her loose. I am grateful now, because that same refusal to "not see" kept her from losing it altogether. Ann, in my opinion, was the frail one. She couldn't take much adversity without feeling responsible somehow. She was the big sister after all, and a great deal of responsibility was dumped in her lap. Our parents were busy working, and Ann had to hold the fort down. Ann never will talk about the demons we lived with, even to this day. She blames all my bad behavior on a severe case of ADHD and no understanding of how to deal with it. I will never try to convince her otherwise. I will gladly take that diagnosis.

Wrong Place at the Wrong Time

At twelve or thirteen years old, drugs became an everyday occurrence. Unfortunately, no one intervened, and I had no outlet for the fury that was building inside me. It wasn't just directed at my dad and Jean. I was mad at the entire world. I wish I could remember the earlier years before that day in the bathroom. Maybe those years with my family were kinder to me, maybe not. By now, I was used to self-soothing. I would steal beer and liquor from home and pain pills from my friends' houses. My friends' parents were getting wise and had started locking their medicine cabinets. The marijuana that was readily accessible in our small town made a good replacement for all the random pills. They were losing their charm and effect anyway. (If anyone tells you that smoking marijuana does not lead to a "Bigger Better High," they are misinformed.) I quickly went from drowning my anguished heart with alcohol and marijuana to taking large quantities of barbiturates and injecting cocaine and heroin into my veins. I was hurting and trying desperately to numb the pain.

One day, I had taken some acid (a psychotic drug) after school and chased it down with alcohol. When I got home, all I wanted to do was fly under the radar, tell my mom I wasn't feeling well, and go straight to bed. When I walked in the door, I saw Ann, Jean, and Sean (the oldest boy). No one else was home.

Even better I thought. I wouldn't have to face my mom's disapproving stare when she knew I was "out of sorts."

On my way to my room, I dropped my purse, and out rolled a tube of mascara. Jean saw it and began to scream at me, accusing me of stealing it from her room. I remained adamant in my denial of any such wrongdoing (although I did in fact steal it from her). She tried to grab it out of my hand, and when I resisted, she began to claw me. She had long nails, unlike the stubs I had from incessant nail biting. Stress will do that!

Since I was inebriated and high, I just wanted to get to my room before either parent walked in. Jean let me know in no uncertain terms that I would get what she felt I deserved from Dad when he got home. But I was going to feel the brunt of her pent-up resentment first. Jean continued her aggressive accusations, and she progressed from her nails to her fists.

I knew I would be blamed, but I decided there was no way I was going to let her report me. If my dad had dragged me into the bathroom again, it would have resulted in a complete unraveling of my soul. I feared my dad, but I also had so much disgust for him at this point. (It was especially sad because I wanted to love my dad. I was just a young, troubled girl in need of a Daddy to protect her, not inflict lasting damage.)

So, I fought back. For what happened next, I don't think even I was prepared. I know my sister wasn't.

Something in me snapped. I remember screaming at the top of my lungs, **"I am going to kill you!"** And I meant it. I ran to the kitchen and grabbed the biggest butcher knife I could find. I came running out of the kitchen with it pointed straight at Jean's hateful heart. We had a large, round dining room table, and I chased her around it a couple of times. I knew if I caught her, I would not hesitate to penetrate that cold heart of hers with all the weight of that steel blade burning in my hand. This was a maddening scene and one of those times my sanity was in question.

Jean made a dash for the stairs. I threw the blade as hard as I could. She rounded the corner and disappeared out of sight, and the knife impaled the wall instead. I remember this made me even more incensed because she had managed to get away. I was not finished allowing my soul to run riot.

I realized she had locked herself in an upstairs bathroom, so with the intensity of a madman I began to thrust the knife as hard and as furiously as I could into the door. At that point, I was no longer in control of this truly horrific event. Jean just happened to be in the wrong place at the wrong time. I am not sure if she has ever forgiven me for this, but I have sincerely asked. Poor Ann also saw the evil that day, and at some point she had the presence of mind to call my parents. Overwhelmed, I fell to the floor outside the locked bathroom and wept, the knife still in my hand.

I honestly don't remember the days following that emotional breakdown. I was sent to the family farm, and Jean had to find a way to process the fact that her little sister had tried to kill her.

I am not sure why my dad didn't just end it for me right then and there. There have been times I wish he had. But I can assure you, God is the One who spared my life that day. And my sister's. I was crazy out of my mind with a level of hatred I could not manage, but all I wanted was someone's attention. I needed to know I was still alive because I truly felt dead. My heart still hurts for Jean. I love her, and I wish I could take back all the pain I caused her.

At sixty-two years old, there is still healing going on in my life. I know we are "made new" in Christ.[17] But some wounds run very deep. Sometimes it is hard to believe that someone as messed up as I was could truly be made new. But Jesus does not lie!

5

THE FARM

I am fuzzy on the timeline, but I know it was summer and soon after the attack on Jean. I remember going to our family farm somewhere in Missouri, just me and my dad and a ranch hand. No siblings. I did hear later that everyone at home was relieved I was absent. Truthfully, I was relieved to get away, and I welcomed the isolation.

I played that sickening scene at the house over and over in my mind. I had shocked myself. I was the girl who brought injured birds and baby rabbits home who had been separated from their mom. I was the girl who, while digging for worms, found a nest of newborn mice.

I took them home and did my best to care for them and keep them alive. I was the tenderhearted one. How could I kill anyone? How could I be the one responsible for my own sister's death? But clearly, I was capable.

I quickly had to find a place to bury all those sickening feelings and emotions. What was happening to me? So much hate and violence and ugliness and wretchedness surrounded me. I had suffered so much abuse. And now I had become the abuser. I didn't suppose I could take much more, so I buried all the horribleness in some deep abyss that accumulated inside of me. Later it would rear its ugly head. Something good had to happen soon before there was truly no turning back from my downward spiral. I desperately needed someone to intervene. And God did in a way I will never ever forget!

Once I settled in at the farm (a large property my parents had purchased, with a house and two barns), I began to find plenty to keep me entertained. There was a horse I could ride if I earned the privilege. She wasn't mine, but belonged to the ranch hand, I think. Her name was Star. I also had a pig named Arnold. There was no one around for miles, except an older couple who lived on the other side of the pasture. I would ride Star for hours, going down to the road (which was a good quarter of a mile away), and then running her as fast as I could back to the barn. After a few sprints, Star and I would take a short swim in the pond, just long enough to get refreshed, and take off again looking for more adventures. I did this until I was told to come in.

I can't even tell you who was there with me during my stay or how long I was at the farm. But something happened between me and my dad that made my "hope meter" begin to rise ever so slightly. God showed up.

I clearly remember that my dad turned out to be the "hero." For the first time ever, I saw and felt the "Daddy" in him. It made me believe there was something redeemable in me, simply because he showed me he cared.

Being at the farm seemed to offer him some breathing space as well. We don't know how others have suffered, or why they act the way they do, without knowing their stories. I don't know what transpired in my dad's home or what abuse he suffered, but it must have been awful too. Evil tends to breed evil, from one generation to the next. What I experienced at the hand of my father was evil. I saw it with my own eyes in that bathroom. As I was bent over the tub, I felt it with every strike of that belt on my body.

My dad was a bully to me for much of my life. But not this day.

Our sow had given birth to a dozen little squealing piglets. One of my farm duties was to take a fishing net, scoop up each piglet, clip its razor-sharp teeth with nail clippers, and put it back with the mom. This prevented the sow from getting cut while her babies nursed. If there was a runt in the litter, it would have to be removed and bottle fed. (Runts are typically not fast enough to get out of the way if the mom turns over.) My favorite thing to do was care for the runts, and I got lucky with this litter. We named the runt Porky. Every pig meant money and provision for our family, so Dad approved of nursing the runts until they were big enough to be put back with the rest of the litter.

A week after they were born, I was enjoying playing "mommy" with Porky, and he and I were playing in the front yard. I ran in the house to get a quick drink. I had been inside about a minute when I heard Porky squealing in a way that told me something was horribly wrong. My heart began to beat so hard I thought for sure it would burst right through my chest. I ran as fast as I could and found him in the jaws of one of our bird dogs. The dogs were chained up, but Porky must have wandered toward them. I was horrified! I grabbed a two-by-four and beat the dog in the head until it released Porky. I picked him up in my arms and noticed a three-inch tear in his belly. His intestines were hanging out, and he started whimpering. That baby pig whimper triggered a flood of tears I could not stop.

I couldn't even scream; my heart was in my throat, and it prevented any sound from coming out of my mouth. I was never one who thought rationally, and this time was no exception. I couldn't run to my dad and the ranch hand. They had been out in the pasture working on the fence. They were too far away, and Porky would bleed to death if I didn't act quickly. So I ran to the house, took one of my mom's dishtowels, and wrapped it around Porky's belly, tying it at the top. Still bawling my eyes out, I ran back outside, hoping somehow the only two people who could help had heard the mayhem and were making a beeline to the house.

When no help arrived, I did the next best thing. Our station wagon was parked in the driveway. I was barely tall enough to see over the dashboard, but that was unimportant. My new baby pig was seriously hurt, and I could not fix him. This revelation made the avalanche of tears seem endless. I laid him next to me on the seat and started the car. Back then people always left the keys in their vehicles. I was in panic mode because Porky had stopped whimpering and just began to shiver. I pushed the gas pedal as far to the floor as I could reach and headed toward my dad. As I drove through a fence and into the tobacco field, I considered what that would mean for me later. But I didn't care. Something I loved was dying. As I got closer to where my dad was working, I could barely see because of my crying. I knew this was not going to end well for me, but I wondered if it would be less brutal since he hadn't started drinking yet. When the station wagon finally came to a halt and before he could yank me out of it, I held up my broken baby pig. Still weeping, I said, "Please, Dad, help him." God performed a miracle that day, and my dad's countenance displayed something that resembled compassion. He looked into my eyes and said, "Let's go back to the house and see what we can do." Tears still fill my eyes whenever I think of this encounter with my dad.

The ride back to the house was in silence except that I was whimpering now. I was emotionally exhausted, and Porky was barely breathing. We got to the house and Dad carried Porky to the kitchen table. He gave me some bourbon and told me to dip my finger in it and put it on Porky's tongue. Oddly enough he began to lick it off my finger. I don't know how much he consumed, but I instinctively understood that it would do the same thing it did for me. Take the pain away. Make him numb.

Soon Dad came back with a spoon, a lighter, fishing string, and a needle. With hands like a surgeon, he sterilized the needle and the spoon, and after gently putting Porky's intestines back into his belly, Dad sewed him up.

The Farm

I think I watched my dad's face more than I watched the stitching. He would look up at me periodically and tell me everything would be okay. I knew he was talking about Porky, but I imagined he was talking about us. I never wanted that moment to end.

About 20 minutes later, the procedure was finished, and Dad made Porky a soft bed in the laundry room where he could recover. Dad explained he had done his best, and it was all up to God now. He even prepared me for the reality that Porky might still die. He told me the reason, but it was in terminology I didn't understand, except he said to watch and see if Porky pooped! That I understood, and I gave my dad a hug (something I never remember doing before this day) and thanked him. For the next several nights, I slept next to Porky. I didn't want to be far from him when he woke up from major surgery. Porky lived a few more days, but then died in his sleep.

I cried again, but this time my tears were a mixture of sadness for the loss of Porky but also gladness for that special moment with my dad—a day I will forever hold very dear to my heart. It is the only one-on-one endearing moment from childhood I remember having with my dad. This was a beautiful gift from God to me. It was meant to give me hope and the courage to go on. This experience was also going to be what God used to remind me some years later that He could do it again. So, in 2016, when my dad was dying from emphysema, and after years of prayer concerning him, God did just that! I will share that experience with you later in this letter.

6

Did Anyone Miss Me?

Summer had come and gone. The visit to the farm had provided an exceptional memory and given me a renewed hope. But my time there came to an end, and it was time to start a new school year. For a few months, things at home seemed almost "normal." A few things had changed. I no longer shared a room with Jean. I was across the hall in my own room, while Ann shared with Jean. I don't think Ann was very pleased about it, but she never made me feel like she disapproved of me. Maybe the incident with the knife was enough to make Ann agree to whatever kept Jean and me apart. No one asked about my time away. They didn't even mention it.

I was hoping they would because I had a doozy of a story to tell. But no one was listening. Isolation once more.

I think they were all embarrassed that one of the Kerry children had serious "problems." I remember trying not to care, and life went on relatively uneventful for a time. Dad and Mom were busy at work, and Ann and Jean pretty much avoided me like the plague. I just reasoned that since they had to watch the younger boys until my parents got home, they didn't have any time to talk with me or even acknowledge me. This was suitable to me for a little while because I experienced a level of "power" that kept all adversaries at bay. I was queen of my own castle, except life was overly mundane, and boredom was definitely my enemy. I was also quite lonely!

Soon the lack of attention from Ann and the condescending looks from Jean were too much. They had banished me from sisterhood status (not that I was ever really part of their "club" in the first place). I came back from the farm without contention in my heart, and I hoped they could at least pretend I belonged. I was really trying hard to hold on to the "warm fuzzies" I felt at the farm. There, I believed what was broken inside me could be repaired and I could be "good" again. But it was harder at home. I don't think Ann meant to hurt my feelings. I think she was under strict orders from the hierarchy (my parents) to give me space. Jean, on the other hand, rejoiced in the fact that she could completely ignore me. Just to taunt me, she would chant, "Willie does not exist! Willie does not exist!"

One evening, my dad arrived home and, to my surprise, did not go straight for the liquor cabinet. Instead he came into the living room, where my little brothers and I were watching cartoons. He had a big silver contraption in his hands. He dismissed the boys to wash up for dinner and told me to come sit next to his chair. For a split second I thought about bolting out of that room as fast as my feet would take me. But I was frozen with fear. It was a very unusual request, and the unknown made me nauseated. What had I done? Had Jean told on me for some transgression? It turned out my dad had talked with some "specialist" about how to deal with a child like me. Whoever the Einstein was suggested he use a pressure cooker as a visual aid as he talked to me about "letting off steam." If I hadn't rolled my eyes during the speech, I might have made it through the evening without incident. Sadly, I made a huge mistake in disrespecting my father's attempt at taking a psychological approach. Although I did not get the standard whipping with his belt, I was deprived of dinner and sent to my room for the night—a punishment I was elated over.

But the second mistake of the night was sneaking out my bedroom window after everyone went to bed. I knew I could find drugs in our neighborhood, and the wound caused by continual rejection was beginning to fester. I had tried so hard to fit in and be what I thought they wanted me to be. But I could never make anyone happy so what did it matter? I carefully used pillows and clothes to make it look like I was still in bed, slipped out the window, and took off to find some comfort elsewhere. The always-on-duty Jean was not about to let me get away with sneaking out to enjoy revelries with friends, so when she realized I was gone, she quickly told my parents. Of course, I was grounded, but not before Dad had to prove once again who was boss! The belt!

As cruel as the beatings were, it was harder for me to cope with the anguish of knowing I was not loved. What father beats his daughter out of love? Not that I remember ever hearing my dad say "I love you" anyway. That night I was given a double portion of the strap, because a member of our church had seen me, and rule number one was, "Never embarrass the family." After all, the Kerry's were loyal members, tithers, and cozy companions of the clergy at St. Margaret's.

THE SHAME GAME

Life went on until one day everything took a turn for the worse. Part of me wishes I could recall fully the details surrounding this devastating incident. So much of it remains a mystery, but the fuzziness doesn't reduce the feeling of being violated. I was fourteen or fifteen at the time. Alcoholism is a relentless spirit that comes to kill, steal, and destroy!

I remember it being a relatively uneventful afternoon. It was a Saturday, I think, because I was out of school. My mom was at work and the other kids were away from the house. I had asked my mom if my friend James could come over and watch TV with me for a little while. He and I were friends from school, and he must have lived close, because he was able to walk to our house. Mom instructed me to keep the visit to no more than an hour, and I gladly agreed. I really liked James and felt honored that he wanted to come over and hang out with me, since he was quite popular with the teenage girls in our school. We were only thirty minutes into our program when I heard my dad's voice outside the back door. It sounded like he was hollering at the neighbor kids, but whatever was happening it seemed to be agitating him. Even though I was sure it had nothing to do with me, that familiar queasiness swept over me. It took only a split second for me to realize that he was either drunk or just really angry. Even though I had my mom's permission to have my friend over, I panicked and told James to make a mad dash up the stairs and out the front door. My heart was pounding so hard that it physically hurt my chest. He came into the living room, his eyes wild with suspicion. He was spewing accusations about me having boys over and doing all sorts of vulgar things. I couldn't tell where one accusation ended and another began, but I lied and said that no one was in the house but me. That was a colossal mistake because he heard the upstairs door slam behind James. My lie on top of the assumed lewd behavior made him even more enraged and set a course in motion that would not only haunt my dreams but lead me into a life of flagrant sexual promiscuity. The indictment continued as saliva spewed through his lips with each remark. I can't remember all of his words, but I will never forget the last thing he whispered close to my ear, before dragging me up the staircase by my hair and shirt: "If you are going to act like a whore, then I will show you what it feels like to be a whore." It was the way he whispered it that sent chills up my spine. After that I have no recollection. Sometimes I wonder if post-traumatic stress disorder is the reason I have blocked so many incidents out.

Where was the "Daddy" who so carefully sewed Porky's little belly back together? Was that reassurance of love just a cruel joke? In the days, weeks, and months that followed, I would knowingly disgrace the family on several occasions. I would deliberately hurt them like they had hurt me, and I was convinced they deserved it. I possessed a relentlessness that could not be tamed. From that point on, I was determined not to allow anything or anyone to break through the iron shell I had constructed over my heart. Sometime later, Jean discovered drugs I had hidden in my dresser drawer. She must have thought this would be the last straw and my parents would have to do something more radical to end the madness we all were experiencing. They did. I ended up in a mental health hospital—a place I never dreamed I would be. I hated my dad for sending me there. Jean was certainly approving of the decision, while Ann was scared for me. My mom made me feel guilty for letting such a thing happen. My dad was eerily quiet about it, but eager to see me leave. The night before being hospitalized, I had a reoccurring dream.

REVELATION DREAM

For years I had an ongoing dream. In this dream, I flew freely with Casper the Friendly Ghost, a cartoon I watched regularly as a young girl. During those late-night escapades, I felt emancipated from "family" and released from the condemnation of my own culpability. I was able to momentarily forget all the senseless damage that had been done. I must have dreamt about Casper once or twice a week as a child. But now I was fifteen and hadn't seen Casper in my dreams for a long time.

I would typically be awakened in my dream by the voice of my favorite ghost. He would beckon me to come out and fly with him. I would hesitate briefly, because I knew if I got caught, it would mean the inescapable strap. But the thought of soaring high above the trees, out of reach of any impending doom, was too tempting, and I could not refuse. I would be ever so quiet as I slipped out of my room, down the stairs, and out the back door. Casper would give me a smile and take my hand. Off we went. I can remember thinking to myself as I was high above the cares of the world, "Where else could I ever feel as free as I do right here, right now?" Casper never let go of my hand, and after a few minutes, he would bring me home. He never said anything more, but I knew he would be back very soon. It was the same scenario dream after dream—until one miserable day, when both my dad and my mom had dealt real blows to my self-worth. They were sending me away. Not to someplace familiar like the farm or maybe to my grandparents, but to a mental institution.

My dream that night started out like any other. But this time, the flight seemed rushed, and I didn't feel the same sense of freedom. I tried to brush it off, but just when I thought I had, Casper looked over at me and let go of my hand (something he had never done before). I began to plummet to the ground, and when I landed, I found myself sitting in a large arena-type room. The atmosphere was very morose, and there was a stench of sulfur in the air. Around me sat hundreds—maybe thousands—of men, women, and children. Each one of them looked almost frozen. Their eyes were locked onto something in the center of the room. If I hadn't seen them breathing, I would have thought they were statues.

Just then I heard a voice. It didn't sound human, even though I understood the words to be English. When I looked, I saw a figure of a man whose face was turned away from me. He was causing quite the commotion, and each person in the arena seemed terrified, except me. He was shooting something that looked like lightning bolts out of the tips of his fingers. They would randomly hit one of the spectators and kill that person on the spot! It wasn't the irrational executions that caught my attention, or even this creature's powerful capabilities (although the whole scene was very distressing). But what he was saying stirred an uneasiness in my spirit. I must have retained the all-important lessons we got in catechism, because this "creature man" was shouting all forms of what I knew to be blasphemy: "God is dead, because I killed Him. I am God now," said the man.

This fiendish ringmaster now demanded my attention, even though he had yet to turn around and face me. He continued attacking the very foundation of my religious upbringing, even though I never cared about my spiritual well-being or the church (aside from my regular visit to the confessional). Right then, something inside me took great offense, and I knew instinctively I had to defend God. (Remember, this is all in my dream.) I stood and began to boldly confront the man's erroneous accusations. I tried to sound brave as I yelled, "Who do you think you are? God is not dead, and you definitely are NOT God." I continued on: "These trifle tricks you play with the lightning flashing from your fingertips are nothing compared to the power God has. You are nothing!"

Right then he spun around with a crazed look. His eyeballs bulged from his head as sweat poured from his hideous face. I instinctively knew it was Satan. But it was also the face of my father on that horrifying night in the bathroom. It was also the same face that dragged me up the stairs. Now I was really frightened. With a trembling voice, I began quoting Bible verses under my breath. I must have paid attention to some of the stories in catechism class, because then I started talking about Daniel in the lions' den: "If God rescued Daniel, surely He will rescue me. Shadrach, Meshach, and Abednego were thrown in the fiery furnace, and they did not get burned. God rescued them." I continued to repeat the truths of these stories to myself. I can't say that courage took over, because I was anything but brave. But knowing these stories somehow helped. But it did agitate this creature-man.

Then Satan pointed his electrically charged fingers at me and blasted lightning bolt after lightning bolt around my head. I was being terrorized all over again, but when he called me by name and told me to come to him, I thought I might crumple out of sheer fear. I panicked, because I was being drawn down to the center of the arena like a magnet and entirely against my will. His defiant stare was menacing, but I couldn't look away. At that very moment, the veil of discernment was opened, and a revelation shook me to my core: It was Satan who beat me so mercilessly in that bathroom. He was simply using my dad. It was Satan who dragged me by my hair up the staircase. I know this may sound twisted, but I really believe my dad loved me. But because of his own unresolved pain, he succumbed to the puppetry of the evil one. Satan wanted me dead, and he was using my dad to accomplish it. Why?

North County Mental "Hell" Institution

The next morning, as if my life of being misunderstood, rejected, and abused wasn't enough, my parents then did the unthinkable—they discarded me. I was fifteen years old, for crying out loud! I had absolutely no idea how to process what was happening as we drove in silence to the mental hospital. Like I had done during so many other unpleasant experiences in my life, I crammed my feelings in the reservoir of my soul, where all the other unsettled, unaddressed, and rotting pieces of my existence went. That reservoir had to be quite deep because it was holding a lot of garbage.

This last fatherly betrayal would thrust me into a life of hell on earth. The hell in my dream was nothing like the angst of my real life. I was being thrown headlong, with no life rope, into a raging sea of desperation. Life was out of control. I was out of control.

My expulsion from the family was now sanctioned. My dad happily provided the boxes for me to pack up all my belongings, and I think I stuffed each box in record time. I understand now why he was so eager to get me out of the house. Whatever measure of horror plagued his dreams and whatever guilt consumed his thoughts, he had decided it was enough. Perhaps he feared I might unleash all the family secrets during my next visit to the confession booth.

I don't remember much about the drive to the hospital. I just remember silence. When I arrived, we were met by the doctor and a large burly nurse named Else. I knew right away I hated her because she had the most condemnatory stare. I knew she wasn't going to tolerate any shenanigans from this little rebellious Irish girl. And since I was already past the point of caring, I purposefully gave her my "you better be prepared for hell on wheels" stare. I locked my squinted eyes on hers and snarled my lip. Truth be told, I was petrified. But I would make sure not a single person knew it—including myself. I wanted to be equipped with ideas for retaliation when the need presented itself. I'm pretty sure I didn't actually intimidate Else.

I was being deserted by my parents at a sanatorium full of crazy people I didn't know. My spirit fought to keep just a piece of my own heart soft and safe, like I was at the farm, but my "hope meter" was on fumes, and there wasn't a chance in this "hell" that I would see relief any time soon. And at the time, this cold, sterile house of misfits is what I assumed I deserved. I still did not want to be there. The induction into North County was a cataclysmic event for me, but I was determined not to cross the threshold quietly.

I must have been daydreaming because I was assaulted by Else's booming voice. She demanded I pay careful attention to the guidelines of my confinement! She was the perfect commandant, with her icy stare and rigid stance. This strategy must have worked for previous detainees, but I wasn't going to be unsettled by it. I had been demoralized enough to last several lifetimes. In some ways, I was looking forward to a not-so-friendly scrap with her. Her manner was so condescending. I can't remember ever observing an ounce of decency in her. Jean would no longer be the unfortunate recipient of all my revulsion. Else would.

For the next hour or so, while Else looked on, the doctor explained the program in detail. I was so focused on his voice that I barely heard a word he said. His tone and expressions revealed such empathy. He seemed to be a genuinely kind man and wanted to make this transition as smooth as possible for me. I was so thankful. I began to daydream as I sat there, and I imagined that the only two people in that room were the doctor and me. I shared all the memories of childhood abuses that were festering in that cistern of mine, and the doctor didn't even blink an eye. He just listened with empathetic ears and compassion in his eyes. When I was finished speaking, he took my hand and very reassuringly told me that everything was going to be all right and that I could come live with him instead.

Woefully, I was jolted back to reality when Else kicked the leg of my chair and demanded I focus on the task at hand. She wanted to get me admitted and to my room. By now, I was exhausted. For this one time and one time only, I agreed with Else. She led the way out of the doctor's office and down a narrow corridor to an undersized room with two single beds and no window. That's all I remember about the décor of my new accommodations at North County.

North County Mental "Hell" Institution

My boxes were stacked on the floor. I sat on the edge of one of the beds, feeling as lost and as vulnerable as any fifteen-year-old could. The musty smell of a cold, concrete basement pervaded the room, and it sent unsettling chills through my entire body. Washed (but stained) sheets were already on the bed, and an old, itchy wool blanket lay folded at the foot of it. I had never in my life felt more defeated.

At that very moment, I was so overwhelmed that the thought briefly crossed my mind to run out of the room screaming for my dad and mom to take me back. I would swear on a stack of Bibles to be the perfect Irish Catholic girl. But I didn't believe I would ever be allowed back into the Kerry clan. The eviction as a daughter and a sister shattered any dream that I could ever be "good" again. Or could ever be forgiven. All those prayers of penance weren't worth a hill of beans. Now all I could hear echoing from my own personal misery were Jean's words, "Willie does not exist."

I wanted to allow the floodgate behind my eyes to open and the tears to flow without restraint. But that was not an option. That degree of control was crucial to my enduring the days of madness, sadness, and anger ahead. I became disconnected, indifferent, and unfeeling. Was this a blessing or a curse? Later it would prove to be both.

I didn't sleep well that first night. I imagined demons, creeping bugs, and uninvited guests making their way to my bed. My roommate, Cindy, was admitted late into the night and never did go to sleep. She sat on the floor with her knees to her chest, rocking back and forth, back and forth. I think she was older than me. I never asked, and she never told, but she was very thin and seemed as fragile as a china doll.

Finally, morning came, and we were both called to breakfast at 7:00 a.m. sharp. Else was the nurse in charge of our corridor, so it was useless trying to skip a meal. I certainly wasn't hungry, and Cindy gave the impression of one who never ate at all. The walls must have been paper thin, because we could hear Else's gruff voice breach every closed door in the hallway. Since it appeared each room's occupants quickly scrambled to their feet and were out the door in less than a minute, we thought it would be best to follow suit.

All the patients, who ranged in age from ten to seventeen, were wearing whatever they slept in, including Cindy and me. There was no time to brush our hair, brush our teeth, or change out of yesterday's attire. Come to think of it, we wouldn't have been able to anyway, because the bathroom and showers were down the hall. Each lavatory was outfitted with something that resembled a mirror. Some sort of aluminum-like paper stuck to the wall. I guess this might have been a blessing in disguise because I really didn't want to see my true reflection anyway. I haven't really tried to understand why, I just know I didn't. Each corridor shared one bathroom and was watched by hall monitors, who made sure no one fought. Apparently, hall monitor was a very prestigious position, given only to those who complied with the program and did the work.

As the weeks went by, I became more and more insolent. I fought often with Else, and since she wasn't allowed to touch me, I felt I had all the power. After the first month, I was still noncompliant with the program. There were many attempts by the staff to find some common ground, but I was simply too angry to cooperate on any level.

I don't remember having much interaction with Cindy, mainly because she was so reclusive. When supper was over and Else had gone home for the night, Cindy would retreat to the confines of her silent world, and I would find my way to the office of the two night orderlies on duty. They were a lot more lenient about letting patients roam the halls at night if we didn't cause a ruckus. I suppose they were therapists in training, but I'm not sure. I only knew they were there for the night shift. My distorted view of reality (I can only attribute it to what happened with my father) told me I could use my body, looks, and charm to influence and manipulate. This mental hospital is where I learned I was good at it.

If I granted a little, I got a little in return. If I granted a lot, I really got my way. Those night orderlies made some serious mistakes—not the least of which were distributing illegal drugs and exchanging sexual favors with their (underage) patients. Here I knew I had all the power. At least until morning.

One night, as I made my way back to my room, I was feeling rather self-assured. I felt I now had significance in my new environment. I also told myself I wasn't going to let what anyone else did affect me emotionally ever again. I would be solid as a rock in my ability to harden myself for what might lay ahead. I would remain unbreakable. I would stay in control! I would soon eat those words.

I opened the door to my room and saw what looked like a bloody ragdoll that had been tossed on the floor next to Cindy's bed. She had found something sharp enough to slice both of her wrists. I immediately lost all resolve and reverted to that whimpering girl whose baby pig had been ripped open and was bleeding to death. I saw pain—deep, dreadful pain. I could see with my mind's eye that Cindy had sunk into that icky, black abyss too. Although I liked her and she was always kind to me, I hadn't allowed myself to care about Cindy (or anyone else, really) prior to this moment. But all that changed, and I panicked.

I needed to quickly find help, but I couldn't scream. No sound would come out of my mouth. In an instant, I flashed back and saw myself sitting in front of a mirror at ten years old, attempting to take my own life. I remembered all the unfathomable anguish that led up to that moment. I realize now that we both had the same formidable enemy, and he wanted Cindy dead too. I was witnessing again the reality of evil.

I was frozen with fear, but finally a blood curdling scream alerted others to my gruesome finding. As they attended to Cindy, I felt ashamed that I had never bothered to ask why she was there.

I never found out what became of her, or even if she lived or died that night. After the paramedics rushed her over to the hospital, I looked over at the two pools of blood that stuck to that hard, dank floor like paste. I ran to the bathroom and threw up.

As I sat next to the toilet, I determined to find a way out of that foul place. The events of the night showed me I was never going to get to the required stage to be released. That meant I was doomed to a life in the state mental health ward. I had to make something happen myself. I blamed North County for Cindy's likely demise. I also blamed myself for not reaching out or trying to be a real friend. I was no better than my parents or Jean or even Ann. I hadn't cared enough to try to understand Cindy's pain. Maybe all she had needed was a hug and some reassurance that someone understood. I loathed the self-importance in me and threw up again.

That night was prolonged. I left all the lights on in my room. The darkness wanted to overtake me, and somewhere inside I just wanted to surrender, even though I had no idea what was lurking beyond the shadows. I was physically tired and emotionally spent. It was time to get out of there. Permanently!

That next morning, I was asked to meet with the doctor. He wanted to help me process my feelings about the tragedy the night before. I told him point-blank that I was leaving. This time Else was not lingering over me, with the unpleasant odor of her perspiration and breath. I believe somehow the doctor knew that the small frazzled string of sanity I was holding on to was about to snap, so he ordered Else to remain outside.

After discussing what had happened, I informed the doctor that I would not go to any more group psychotherapy sessions or participate in the program. I didn't care what the repercussions were. The doctor listened and offered an alternative to group therapy. Basically, it was solitary confinement. But after he explained it, I agreed to go, and I was dismissed.

Between North County and the hospital is an underground tunnel that supposedly was used as a bunker during the war—it was never explained to me which war. It was quite big, and there was a long passageway made with concrete that also made the perfect tornado shelter. The Midwest has lots of tornados. Maybe not as many as other states, but we often experienced violent storms. But that day I used the tunnel for something different. One of the day orderlies took me down there with a bucket of paint brushes and different paint colors.

For the next two weeks, I spent my days (minus mealtimes) painting the tunnel wall. I felt liberated and secure down there. Although it was quite dingy and musty, there was enough light to paint. I looked at this sizeable piece of wall that had been measured out for me to paint. I could paint whatever I wanted on this canvas the size of a truck. I thought about where I wanted to be—a place without a human being in sight. What came to mind was the album cover of a band called "Yes." The album was "Tales from Topographical Oceans," and the cover art was a landscape of a waterfall under the stars.

So that's what I painted. I wonder if it is still there today, almost fifty years later.

I completed my depiction of isolation, so it was time to begin the program again. I am sure the doctor and Else thought I had been given enough time to think through any objections I might have had. I indulged them both by confirming that I was indeed "restored to rational wellness." But I planned all along for that to be my last night at this mental institution (or any institution for that matter).

I was going to have my night-shift buddies leave the front door unlocked after lights-out. Nonconformity called from the other side. It was beckoning me to renounce the lies of my captors and embrace my own truth and my own way through that single unguarded door. So, at half past ten, I took only what would fit in my backpack and quietly opened the door to my room.

Cautiously, I made my way to the front door. I knew the door would be ajar because I had too many lascivious tales that would have destroyed the two orderlies' careers. Looking back, I should have exposed their shameful treatment of a minor, but at the time, I saw them as my saving grace and the only redeeming thing in that mad house. They also made me feel significant and attractive. Besides that, I couldn't escape without them.

North County Mental "Hell" Institution

When I rounded the corner that led to the door and out to freedom, who would also be heading out the door but Else herself. She had stayed late working on another admit. I think we startled each other, but she made the first move without delay and grabbed me by the arm, demanding I explain myself. I reacted on impulse, and with the tenacity of a two-year-old, I kicked nurse Else in the shin as hard as I could and then ran. I ran out the door as fast as I could, and I ran until I was depleted of all my oxygen. I heard the sirens go off in the distance and hid in a hollowed-out log that had quite a bit of shrubbery around it. Trying hard to overcome my fear of snakes and other creeping things, I wedged myself in. I was panicking and trying not to hyperventilate, but I wasn't having much success. I was so scared of being heard. I held my breath until I couldn't any longer. Then as slowly and quietly as I could, I exhaled and filled my lungs once again. I did that over and over for what seemed like hours but was only a few minutes. Then the sirens ceased, and all was quiet again.

I was eager to get out of that tree stump and check myself for leaches or ticks or anything that might be stuck to me. For the life of me, I can't remember what happened next except that I started walking in the direction opposite of the asylum. Someone picked me up once I made it to the road. They drove maybe thirty minutes and eventually dropped me off at a park where tents a mile wide had been set up. It turned out to be the site of a three-day croquet tournament, which was just a three-day beer-drinking, pill-popping, and pot-smoking party with a bunch of college kids.

What took me by surprise was recognizing a friend and former next-door neighbor growing up. Gary was as surprised to see me as I was him, and I think for a moment he wanted to send me back home. I was still only fifteen, and this was not a responsibility he wanted to assume. But he also knew bits and pieces of my nightmarish childhood and chose to let me stay if I promised not to participate in any drug use. He knew there was an overabundance of pills circulating through the festival. He instinctively knew I had been through something traumatic and didn't want me searching for an antidote to whatever was plaguing me. He also knew how vulnerable I was. But Gary wasn't opposed to me drinking, so drink I did. It was a great weekend, and for the first time in an awfully long time, I felt somewhat normal (or at least as normal as anything I had experienced in a while). I was completely accepted for who I was, even though it was almost all bravado. I was free! For now.

Most of the college kids that were there knew I was Gary's friend, so they were extra nice to me. One of the croquet player's girlfriends let me rest in her tent. I didn't realize until that moment how zapped I was emotionally. So much had transpired in the previous few days, not to mention the previous few years, and now I was sitting in this comfortable and nicely decorated tent. I began to laugh. Then I started to cry and laugh at the same time. It continued for what seemed like hours, but I didn't care. This was an unusual emotional moment for me, and I wasn't concerned with who might hear, because it seemed to loosen some of the inward shackles that held me captive.

I wondered if I was a fugitive, and that thought brought only amusement and more laughter. I was sure I escaped from "everlasting" captivity. You can bet nurse Else would have been the one to lock the door and throw away the key.

Again, laughter and lots of it. No more tears were necessary.

I can't remember how long my incarceration lasted, several months, I think. And although I may not have received an official pardon from North County, I didn't care. I felt free. Suddenly, a revival pitched its tent inside my soul, and I danced around completely oblivious to anything external.

Once the hilarity of the moment had passed, I caught my breath and began to think back on the different seasons in my life. I had a strong desire, almost an urgency, to recall times, people, and places that had brought happiness and wonder into my life. I needed to remember. How crucial it is to remember the diamond in the rough moments. Remember those times and people who made you feel like you belonged. I needed my saneness back. It didn't take very long before my favorite place from all my childhood memories came flooding back into my mind.

There's No Place Like Home

Some of my most treasured memories are from my grandparents' farm in Kansas. These were my mom's parents, and although I didn't escape some hard knocks there a time or two, it was certainly not to the degree I was used to at home. My memories of that place are fond and easy for me to recall, even if they are in bits and pieces. I love to picture all the many wonderful times there, because it produces a little mischievous giggle and a ginormous smile. The Kansas farm was truly home to me, more than any other place when I was a child. I wish I could have shared this wonderful place with my children and let them grow up there as I did. But after I left home and after my grandpa died, that sanctuary—where I felt so sheltered and loved—became just a memory.

The first word that comes to my mind is "distraction." With aunts, uncles, cousins, and grandparents around, there were lots and lots of wonderful distractions. I chased headless chickens (an odd but familiar game to anyone raised on a farm), fed the cows, and spent the wee hours of the morning with my grandpa, better known as Pap, and Tuffy, his loyal livestock chasing dog. Together, Pap and I would drop salt blocks off the farm truck throughout the pasture, and on occasion, he would give me the affirmative wink, which meant I could hop off and give it a quick lick myself. As soon as I was back in the truck, he would say, "So, how did it taste?" I would say with the most disagreeable face, "Ugh, salty!" And we would both break out in a cackle that only my Pap could extract from within me. Somehow, I thought those salt blocks were going to magically taste good one day. Maybe that's why Pap laughed so hard.

Once back in the barn, he would pull up a rickety old three-legged stool and cheerfully plop me down on it while he milked the cows one by one at a snail's pace—all the while whistling a cheerful tune. I was never happier. I would have sat there all day if it meant just the two of us engaged in this undisturbed and blissful existence.

There were wild kittens that I tried endlessly to catch, but to no avail. But as soon as they saw Pap carrying that tin milk bucket, they interpreted it as a "come and get it" announcement. The kittens came out of everywhere, from the tiniest crack in the barn doors and the very tip top of the hay lofts.

They crept closer until Pap pointed the cow's tit at the motley crew and shot them some fresh milk. He didn't bother to aim carefully, but deliberately covered them with the welcomed indulgence. What an amusing sight to watch this feline frenzy, as they wound up in a big ball of fur, licking each other clean.

My Pap gave me moments like this often—tender mercies that set him apart forever in my mind and heart. There I sat in goulashes five sizes too big, a coat that gobbled me up, and a ball cap that covered my eyes and part of my nose. I just remember the cap smelling of Pap's hair paste and the feed grain that he stored in the silo. It was a Norman Rockwell picture-perfect scene. I was in the presence of one who loved me so completely, in whose care I knew I was safe and secure.

How I would love to relive those days with my grandpa Pap. There were many treasured times with this beloved man, but with him mornings were always my favorite. I think because I knew he chose me to get up before the rooster crowed to set out on these marvelous adventures. I relished each moment.

He certainly wasn't at a loss for grandkids to choose. There were seven of us Kerry kids along with ten other cousins at that time who were just as eager to share in Pap's early-morning adventures.

We generally didn't make the drive to Kansas unless there was a family social event that included fishing and beer for the men and chatter and cooking for the women. I'm pretty sure there was more chatter than cooking, but by suppertime, they had somehow put together a great meal.

We kids were basically free to roam the pastures, walk the gravel roads looking for box turtles, ride the horses (if we didn't fight over them), and create our own little wonderland of exploration. We would play "King of the Hill" where an old abandoned cistern sat. We dared each other to climb to the tip top of the silo. Pap would try to sound harsh when he caught us up there and made us get down. But we just giggled. He didn't have a mean bone in his body. Pretending to come down, we'd shoot right back to the top again. Although a fall would have been painful, Pap pretended not to notice and never chastised our disobedience. I guess he figured we might have to learn the hard way.

Most of the time I played with my cousins Mindy and Lyla. We were "three amigos" with a propensity for trouble. Lyla's dad (my uncle) was also very violent and harsh with her. I don't know to what extent; I just knew we had a great deal in common that bonded us. Mindy was the shy one, but she desperately wanted to belong. Her mother (my aunt) tried drinking her inner demons away until they finally became too persuasive. She succumbed to suicide. Lyla and I really loved Mindy, and Mindy loved us too. It was her ability to love unconditionally and completely that was so attractive. So, we set about to create as many pleasant memories as we could at the farm. We were inseparable.

One of my favorite memories of us occurred during the winter. There were three bedrooms upstairs, all with no conventional heat. We girls got one of them. We would all snuggle as close as we could under a heap of quilts and one electric blanket until we were as toasty as breakfast biscuits right out of the oven. But come morning, it would be a very cold race downstairs.

Pap would rise even earlier on these bitter winter mornings to gather wood for the only wood-burning stove we had. But soon the living room was as welcoming as he was. Any minute there would be an onslaught of grandkids making a mad dash to the only room that had been thawed out! Each one of us would be vying for the warmest spot on the floor, but it was a childish and delightful game the cousins played. This was an era that would cement in my mind and heart the unconditional love of family. It was an occasion for commemorating, and I personally wasn't about to let a single opportunity for this uncomplicated camaraderie to slip by.

Being at the farm with my grandparents almost made up for all the good experiences stolen from me at home. Even though Jean was still quite bossy and wanted to maintain her "Willie police" status, she was overruled by my grandparents and aunts. I never gave her much mind there. I believe my relatives knew how difficult life was for me at home so, in those moments, they acted as my own personal buffer. Jean's attempts to assert her self-designated authority over me were shot down. Dad also kept his distance because he knew he was outnumbered.

The few times I remember him trying to locate me after too many drinks, my grandma would hide me in the kitchen cupboards. When my dad would come in the farmhouse hollering for me, she would make up some excuse. I don't remember what she told him, but whatever it was, he sheepishly acquiesced and left. Apparently, he had no choice and knew it! I wish I could remember her words, but all I know is that I was so grateful for them. Once she freed me from my super-secret hiding place,

Grandma would send me off with my favorite aunt to play. Out of sight, out of mind.

We had lots of extended family there in Kansas, but one family was everyone's favorite. My Uncle Ben and Aunt Rae were my grandmother's cousins, but they were Walkins (my mother's maiden name), and that's all that mattered. They lived in a farmhouse about a mile away, and we often walked or rode horses over there. They had several children including some adopted. These precious Walkins loved us kids and let us stay as long as we liked, especially the "three amigos." We loved to spend time at the lake on Uncle Ben and Aunt Rae's property. It was also a favorite fishing and drinking hole of my dad and uncles.

I was reminded recently by my cousin Lyla of a time at the lake when I saved her life and Mindy's life. She told me she will never forget that day. It was also a day when my dad showed a little bit of protectiveness toward me. That's one of the reasons I'll always remember it too.

It was during one summer when we were all spending time at the lake. It must have been July 4th or some other holiday, because all the cousins from my mom's seven siblings were there. Lyla's family had to travel from Arizona, so it had to have been something special, or my uncle (who seemed to hate everything fun) wouldn't have driven that far. We were all on the lake swimming and having a wonderful time.

My dad and I had been keeping our distance from each other. I was protected by the familial buffer, and it was a good thing, because the men were showing no restraint when it came to the amount of alcohol consumed. My Uncle Jay, Mindy's dad, was one of my favorites. He was always kind to me, and even though he acted like a "big dog" around Dad and the other uncles (key word is "acted"), he was really a timid teddy bear. He did, however, indulge in alcohol, but he never demonstrated aggressive tendencies. That was his wife's job. But when Aunt Julie wasn't drinking, she was as kind and docile as my uncle.

That afternoon, Uncle Jay was out in the motorboat, fishing along the opposite shore. Dad and the others were on the shore seeing who could outdo the rest, regardless of the topic of discussion. Mindy, Lyla, and I were floating on top of the water fairly far away, making shapes of the clouds and talking about boys (of course). That's when we heard yelling. It startled all three of us, and we turned to see what all the commotion was about.

I could see my dad and mom (and the others on shore) yelling and frantically waving their hands. My dad looked panicked and angry, and it scared me. I wondered what I had done and how long I would be able to tread water, until something made me turn and look behind me. From that moment on, everything went into slow motion. All I could see was the bow of the motorboat almost on top of us. It was so close that there was no way we could swim out of the boat's path fast enough. Those propeller blades were coming for us.

My uncle had been drinking and wasn't paying attention. He drove that boat right over the top of us. In a split second, I grabbed the hair of both cousins and pulled them under the water and under my body, to protect them from the propeller's destruction. All I remember was a thud and the sound of a motor shutting down. When I heard that, I released my cousins, hoping I hadn't drowned them in my attempt to save them.

All three of us broke the surface of the water, gasping for air since we hadn't had the chance to take in any on the way down. Both girls were crying and swimming as fast as they could to shore. I froze. My eyes were still fixed on shore. I was studying my dad's demeanor and face. I was still wondering if, somehow, I was to blame for something completely unbeknownst to me.

By then, my aunts were in the water helping Mindy and Lyla to shore, checking every inch of their bodies for any indication of serious injury. I watched this scene as though I was not really in it, and all my senses seemed hazy and disconnected. I could hear all kinds of expletives coming from my dad's mouth, but when I realized they were not directed at me, my spirit seemed to rejoin my body, and I felt like it was safe to meet the others on shore.

I swam back. Although I was not unscathed, my injuries were minor. I felt bad for Uncle Jay because he would never have intentionally hurt a fly. But he was being berated and threatened with physical harm. It went past the point of reasonable admonition. It was a terrible mistake in judgment on his part, but after that, I never again witnessed him drink and drive.

I will always remember seeing my dad act terrified for the life of his daughter. He was worried about me! I don't remember him coming to check on me after, but somehow just the fact that he was rattled made me feel significant. I wish I could say this event was a lesson to everyone involved on the destructive nature of alcoholism, but unfortunately the generational curse continued.

While the farm is no longer a place where I joyfully chase headless chickens, lick salt blocks, or watch wild kittens with Pap, I will forever hold these memories in my heart. My days spent there were heaven on earth for me, filled with love, care, and a sense of certainty. And once my eyes were opened through faith in the Lord Jesus Christ (at age twenty-four), my time on the farm with Pap would become a picture of something even more valuable. Grace and Mercy.

Angels Unaware

I know that most people can outline the years of their lives with clarity. They remember times and dates and can recall them easily. But my life has never been like that. Now, as a follower of Christ, I know those (what I call) lost years were a gift. Jesus was protecting me from any more damage to my already fragile spirit.

After my escape from the mental health institution, my life, once again, journeyed down a dark road. At age sixteen and free from all parental expectations and authority, I was propelled into a world I really knew nothing about. Without God's direct intervention, I would have ended up dead or even more deeply scarred than I already was. There have been several noteworthy angelic moments in my life, but a few have been extremely significant. These experiences may be difficult for some to believe, and some are embarrassing to tell. But they are part of my story, and they are important.

I sometimes stayed with school friends or other acquaintances. I tried hard to attend my high school, and most of the time my attendance was good. But I was disillusioned with education, and I certainly didn't want any authority figures directing my life. Once again, I was in serious trouble with drugs. The milder ones were again losing their charm and effect. It didn't come as a surprise to me when I quickly wore out my welcome and was asked to leave. With my options limited, I slept in parks, laundromats, and 24-hour restaurants. I had no direction and felt alone in the world.

This is when I began to experiment with LSD, snorting cocaine, and taking other psychotic drugs. After that, shooting cocaine became my preference. After that, heroin. I realize that not all drug users go to the extent I did, but I was on a downward spiral, and I didn't care. New drugs were circulating, and their effects were guaranteed to surpass all the others. I was wooed by their ability to ease my crippling fears and immense emotional pain. In my mind, using them wasn't even a choice anymore.

They were who I had become. I wasn't even concerned about what concoction filled the syringe.

One night, I found myself in an unfamiliar place with unfamiliar people. A man, really Satan's marionette, was making his way around a smoky room. He was going person to person, filling and refilling syringes with venom—either heroin or some generic version of it.

With the same defiled needle, he pierced the veins of his victims and watched with delight as their eyes rolled back in their heads and their bodies collapsed to the floor. It was my turn. I don't recall being afraid, which tells me I was probably already high on something else.

When I woke up, I remember being completely exposed. My clothing had been torn and tossed to the side, and I was in the middle of a crude and revolting scene. I knew I had been raped. I couldn't move or leave, even though something deep down inside me said, "Run for your life, Willie, run for your life." I can't even remember who I was with or how I got there. I share this with you so you understand the depth of my own depravity and the power of the enemy. And to say that no matter how deep the sin is in our lives, God loves us and wants to save us. He died for this scene I just described. That fact absolutely astounds and amazes me.

During this next five-year period, if I were high, I could forget I was damaged goods. After all that had happened at home in my childhood and during adolescence, I was drowning in misery. I needed a "cure" for my miserable existence.

I foolishly allowed the drugs to become a form of deliverance. But it was all one big sinister lie. Drugs alleviated nothing. Instead, they tormented me.

I wanted so badly to be a "good girl." One that a daddy would love, a sister would cherish, and my own heart would recognize as worthy. But I didn't have the courage to confront the truth of what I had become, and it was killing me. My enemy and yours, Satan, will always attempt to make us feel shame and guilt. We must choose to reject that lie. It is a choice.

I was in such a precarious place. I believe God chose me to be His, and He continued to pursue me and used even His angels to bring me back to Him. I didn't recognize His hand in the moment, but I knew that every time I was about to step off a precipice into the dark (like in the scene just mentioned), a stranger would swoop in and rescue me. I would find myself in a strange home, fully clothed, sleeping on a safe couch. I love that even though we have free will to choose whether to follow

God or not, He knows the world is terribly broken and He graciously sends His angels to watch over us.

I believe my earliest angelic encounter was when I was sixteen. I had hitched a ride to Wyoming and found myself in the Yellowstone National Park area. I had a backpack with a few clothing items, granola bars, my toothbrush, toothpaste, and some hotel shampoos. With no job and no money, I had to steal these items. Although I am not proud of it, I did what I had to do in order to survive. I would find a gas station or convenience store and use its bathroom as my own personal spa. I would pull out my shampoo and wash my hair, face, and private areas with the icy cold sink water. I dried off with paper towels. If I got lucky, the bathroom had one of those handy dryers attached to the wall. I welcomed the warmth. I also loved those 24-hour laundromats. I had to get sleep somehow, and I just figured that most people who chose to do their washing in the middle of the night were surely harmless. So I fluffed my backpack as best as I could, stretched out on a bench, and closed my eyes for what I hoped would be a dreamless night.

I had been in the Yellowstone area for a couple days. I think it was the weekend, and I was getting tired and lonely. I had walked for miles, and the excitement of my gypsy persona was wearing off. I needed a plan.

I didn't want to go back to my hometown in Missouri. I didn't have a chance there. Too many bridges had been burned, and I had not spoken to any of my family since my escape from North County. As far as I know, North County never reported me missing and my family never came looking for me.

Soon I came across a section of town that presented a plethora of bars. I had gone days without drugs. I had mostly seen trees, dirt roads, an occasional stream, and a few hiking passersby. My head was clearer than it had been in a long time, but as I approached the entrance to one of the bars, my heart and mind began to race.

I talked to myself: "Just keep walking, Willie. Don't stop!" But the desperate part of me argued back: "But what if you meet someone kind and are invited to stay a day or two? Surely not everyone has impure motives." I told myself I wouldn't drink this time. Then again, one drink wouldn't hurt. I'd been so good. I was so tired of walking. Maybe I deserved a drink. I sure was lonely. But I was also cashless. Then I remembered some of my old tricks.

All of a sudden, I was at a crossroads. Fear and insecurity reared their ugly heads, and I needed to choose how I was going to deal with them. It was getting late, and I was in need. If I chose to go in—and truth be told,

I wanted to—I knew I would need to put on whatever mask I needed to get what I wanted. Or, I could keep walking and find a secluded place to sleep once I was past the temptation.

I made my decision. I gave in once again to the lie of the enemy and made my way inside. The Willie that was able to assault a nurse and run out into the dark and into the unknown and the Willie that manipulated and captured the affections of two male night orderlies came flooding back to the surface. I was full of bravado. I knew it would get me a few drinks and some company, at least for a while. What I would do or where I would go when the party was over, I did not know.

I can't remember all the details of this night. I flirted my way into the likings of some local boys, and soon the tequila started flowing. I remember winding up at the piano, inebriated enough to try to pull off the pretense that I was musically proficient. Although I loved the piano (mainly because my mother was very gifted and could play anything and everything), I couldn't play a lick but chopsticks. Here I was, fingers on the chipped and incomplete keys, "playing" for the crowd as though it were a normal weekend gig. I went so far as to take requests—mainly Irish folk songs, because that genre of music was like the Pledge of Allegiance in the Kerry home. Some words I knew. Most I didn't. But I played and sang anyway. Almost all the patrons were as drunk as I was, so it probably sounded as good to them as it did to me. What happened next was unexpected and unexplainable, but I truly believe God sent His angels to rescue me.

It was very late into the night or possibly early morning when several of the regulars came over to the piano and sat down beside me. I'm certain these were the same "lads" who now wanted some compensation for all the drinks they bought me. I was not a light drinker. I could put down shots of tequila and maintain an upright position as well as any Kerry, so I'm sure I cost them a pretty penny. And it wasn't going to go unrewarded, or so they thought! These boys insisted I join them for some coffee at the local 24-hour diner. They also assured me they could be trusted and that their intentions were, of course, innocuous. I wasn't a very good judge of character after my third or fourth shot, so I agreed to go. As I was getting up to leave, four large men approached the piano just in time to tell my newfound "friends" to take a hike. What was happening? Those boys were my only hope of a hot breakfast, but apparently, I wasn't going anywhere with them.

You had to be in the presence of these "mountain men" to really get a feel for the authority they possessed. The boys attempted to overrule the ZZ Top-looking characters, but it wasn't long before all of them tucked their tails between their legs and made a beeline for the door. Before I knew it, I was sober, sitting at the bar drinking coffee and having a conversation with these angels. Not only did they rescue me from a date with darkness, but they comforted me with words of healing, hope, and even a future. I certainly hadn't entertained the idea that my life could be something wonderful, at least lately. But they were resolute in what they were preaching. My life had simply been a day-by-day journey, and I had tried to avoid thinking about those abstract concepts. I hadn't wanted to get my hopes up.

They told me they had a room where I could stay until I decided what my next step would be. I left with them, feeling unusually convinced I was in the care of someone fantastic. Any trepidation I should have had (there were four of them and one of me), I simply didn't. We drove for quite some time, disappearing deeper and deeper into the mountains. All I could think about was that I was tired of walking with no real direction and tired of running from all the demons that wanted to torment me. But mostly, I was tired of me. I had finally worn myself out, and I just wanted rest. Real, both-eyes-closed rest! I couldn't remember the last time I had let myself fall into that kind of deep, undisturbed sleep, but it was all I desired right then.

Finally, we arrived at a quaint log cabin. From the outside, it reminded me of an old shack from one of the "Gunsmoke" episodes. I saw a fire pit in the front yard and a rocker on the porch. The rocker looked like a giant spool of thread (without the thread) that had been cut in half. It was an odd-looking piece of furniture, but it was clearly a favorite of my new friends. At least I was hoping they were friends, not foes.

Inside the décor was a classy mountain chic. It seemed tidy and clean, and instantly I felt at home. If they were angels (and I do believe they were), I can imagine God telling them that they better not be slobs or He would send a tidier group. I can't say I know how the spiritual realm operates, but I just know it does. The dining room table was massive. The chairs were meant for giants. I was Edith Ann in her oversized rocker. If you haven't heard of her, look her up on Google. All the furniture was made from logs just like the ones that built the cabin. To this day I wish I could remember my rescuers' names, but those have completely eluded me at this point.

The five of us sat together chatting about my outrageous adventures. I was offered a nightcap of good old-fashioned hot cocoa, and within a few minutes the warmth of the cocoa mixed with the smell of pine and logs took me back to those wonderful times in Colorado as a child. My heart slowed to a peaceful pace, and my eyes began to close for what I hoped would be a restful escape from my troubles. I felt as though I might sleep undisturbed forever. I quickly made my way up a ladder into a cozy loft. I let myself be engulfed by a bed of pure fluff. The feeling of sheer security in this moment made me hope I would never be asked to leave.

The next morning, or should I say afternoon, I woke to the smell of bacon frying and the sound of chatter and laughter downstairs. I sat up to see if I had been dreaming or if I truly had been protected and cared for by four unusual men. I was starving, so it didn't take long before I found myself downstairs, scarfing down a huge breakfast of pancakes, bacon, fruit, and eggs. Did these guys do anything on a small scale? I don't remember how long we talked or what was said, except that after we were done, I knew I had to go back home to Missouri to finish school. Whatever they said, it gave me the confidence that it wasn't too late. Something inside me told me they weren't just talking about school.

Do you know what is odd and will sound too "mysterious" to believe? I don't know how I got home. I know we didn't drive, and I would remember if I had gotten on a plane. But somehow, I was transported from a remote cabin in the Wyoming hills to a friend's apartment back home. However it happened, it was a miracle. And I know from Scripture that God can miraculously move people. He did it for Enoch, Elijah, and Philip. It's not outside the realm of possibility that He did it for me too.

I did return to school to finish out my junior year, but I often reflected with great fondness on my time in the woods with my mountain men rescuers.

I was tired of being in a small town where everyone knew my business. I spent a lot of energy trying to avoid running into any of my family members. The judgment was crippling, and I just wanted to be able to breathe. One day I was on my way to a big party at one of the more remote parks in the area where all the high school kids went to "party." I must have been driving a boyfriend's car because I didn't have one of my own. But instead of blasting the radio as I drove and anticipating the time of unabashed revelry, I sat in the quiet and felt very somber. Maybe my brief stay in Wyoming and the words spoken over me were still tugging at my heart. For whatever reason, I really didn't want to go, and as I was about to approach the park, I looked up into the sky and said, "God, I just want to be a good girl." This simple prayer was heard from heaven, and as I look back now, I can imagine God giving His angels a knowing wink and saying, "You heard her. Go!"

So, once I got to the park, I was offered all the usual remedies for whatever ailed you. But this time I didn't feel the need to self-soothe. I wandered around for a while, realizing that I needed to get as far away from this scene as possible. I felt a presence there I didn't understand, but it gave me the courage and strength to leave.

Throughout the rest of high school, I continued to struggle in so many areas. But I did my best to stay busy by working at a Pizza Hut. And I avoided certain places and people. Finally, I graduated with the rest of my class. That was a miracle all by itself, and it was an accomplishment I was going to value even if no one else did. I did have to serve ten detentions after graduation if I wanted my paper diploma. Looking back, I think it was the principal's way of having the last word where Willie was concerned. Only my mom came to my graduation.

After graduation, all my friends went off to college, and I went to live with my boyfriend and two of his friends and their girlfriends in the college dorm. I was the only one whose grades hadn't allowed me to go to college. I couldn't have afforded it anyway. While they went to class and studied to do great things, I kept the dorm room tidy, made sure there were plenty of snacks, and tried to find ways to ease my boredom. Insecurity raged inside me, but I was good at hiding it.

I had been relatively clean and sober since my visit to Wyoming, but when we crossed the threshold into the college scene, there was an instant temptation to belong and fit in. In no time at all, a new beast was introduced to our little small-town group—pure liquid cocaine. Absolute fear gripped my entire being because I knew the addictive dangers that awaited me. I wanted to have the power to say no, but I was still plagued by the need to belong, especially in this environment. It was a Friday night, and one of our friends had come back to the room with some sort of locked chest. In it was a backpack full of new syringes, alcohol, and tourniquets. He locked the dorm room door and put a "Do Not Disturb" sign on the outside knob. That meant "party time," and everyone was eager to see what this night would hold for all of us. I was afraid, but I didn't let on. I knew this was not going to end well, but the peer pressure was immense. I felt that if I didn't go along with the crowd, even though they were my friends, I would be asked to leave. And where would I go? A nonparticipant was assumed to be a potential "narc," no matter how strong the relationships were. I didn't want that label. I would rather die. So I almost did.

One of the guys filled a syringe with the cocaine, tied his arm off with the tourniquet, and proceeded to discharge the contents of the vial into his vein. Then he did the same to his girlfriend, and before I knew it, we were all taking turns. We might as well have had loaded guns cocked and pressed against our temples. No one really knew what they were doing or what the result would be. The effect of this pure cocaine was euphoric. And it was instantly addictive. It gave the illusion of unadulterated joy. I can never remember a time that I felt so much pleasure and exhilaration. Of course, it was all a drug-induced delusion —a strategic lie from the enemy. But I believed it was real. I believed it was good, and after trying it, I believed I couldn't live without it. The effects lasted for maybe an hour. All I could think about was when it would be my turn again. Up until that point, Satan had been unsuccessful in any attempts to kill me. But he was ramping up his efforts.

That next Monday, the boys headed to class, and two of the girls went back to our hometown where they would start community college. I was left in the dorm room alone because I had nowhere to go and no place to be. I didn't fit in anywhere. I instantly wanted that enraptured feeling again. This time my struggle was loneliness. So many uncertainties surrounded my status as a nonstudent female living in a male dorm on campus. I didn't even realize it was against College dorm protocol for me to be there. I was simply instructed by my boyfriend not to leave the room unless he was with me.

I knew where the syringes were hidden, but I needed to find that liquid thrill that made my whole world blissful and carefree. The temptation was impossible to resist: "Every care you have in the world can be erased in just minutes, Willie." The demonic influence was so strong. "Willie, you will feel remarkable. Willie, you need this. You are an addict, but it's okay, because you are in a safe and controlled environment. Go ahead. No one will notice just a little is missing."

And so I fervently searched the dorm room. I overturned mattresses, poured out drawers, and emptied backpacks. Every ounce of decency in me was gone. I was fully committed. I found the locked chest under one of the beds. I didn't hesitate. I remember my fingers bled as I desperately pried open the chest. This race for freedom was about to end terribly.

I quickly took two syringes and the container of liquid bliss and put them deep inside my purse. I headed out. I didn't know where I was going, but I was desperate to get there. I found myself walking through the cafeteria. I'm not sure why. Maybe because I secretly hoped to be stopped and rescued from sure wreckage. No one reached out. I don't know why I thought someone would. So I continued to search for a super-secret place. I wasn't fully prepared for the cravings. Something deep inside was ravenous. I knew I had to find a place soon, because my body began to quiver and ache. The urgency to inject was overpowering. I tried desperately to control the battle now raging in my mind. The voices were screaming at me to hurry, as though if I didn't make this happen now, I would shatter into a million pieces right where I stood. Feeling as though I was stripped of my free will, I frantically ran into the closest room I saw, which was a women's bathroom. I had forgotten the tourniquet, so I stripped off my white sweater, leaving myself bare and exposed. I tied off my arm as tightly as I could and filled both syringes. I believe the demons who had been conspiring to destroy me were hovering over me, wringing their hands, salivating in anticipation of capturing another soul for all eternity.

By the time I was finished, I had stabbed myself several times in each arm. I was later found unconscious, partially naked, with a needle still dangling from one of two hideously bruised arms. I don't know who stumbled upon this sick scene. When I came to and tried to speak, I couldn't put any understandable words together. As if from the outside looking in, I saw the state I was in and began to weep. I willingly submitted myself to this person's care. I remember nothing more than leaving the college and arriving once again back in my hometown. How had I gotten there? Who were these strangers who kept helping me? Certainly they had to be angels! They always seemed to be there precisely when I needed them the most.

It was time for a serious change. I wanted to leave Missouri behind, along with everyone who knew me. I stayed with a girlfriend from high school, and she helped me the next few months. I reconnected with some other high school friends I had met my senior year. They asked if I wanted to move to San Francisco with them, and it took less than five seconds for me to say, "California? Sure!" We packed up a small car with three girls, one hitchhiker, and all our belongings. The anticipation of seeing the beautiful Bay Area made up for the uncomfortable ride in the sardine can on four wheels.

I was seventeen and desperately wanted to make something of my life. I figured somewhere across the Golden Gate was just as good a place as any other. We initially stayed with the sister of one of the girls in our group. She lived in Pittsburg, just outside San Francisco, California. Within the first month of being submerged in the West Coast lifestyle, I met a guy named Robert at a dance club one night. We danced all night and the next night and the next weekend. Satan was clever with this one, because Robert's words eased every insecurity I had. It wasn't long before I moved in with him and his two roommates. It's funny how our pasts can continue to affect our present lives, no matter how far removed we are geographically. I knew the most effective way to get what I wanted. Just like I had done with the two orderlies at North County. So I was rewarded with a roof over my head and food to eat.

I liked Robert and enjoyed his company. At first, he was fun and funny and seemed to really want me in his life, so much so that he invited me to move back to his hometown of Missouri. I almost couldn't believe my ears. Of all the states, he had to be from Missouri! If Robert had said Gladstone, I would have bolted as fast as my thumb could hike me out of there. But he said Springfield instead. That was better. And what were my options at that point? I found out the girls I traveled with in the first place had turned out to be lesbians, and the place we would be staying was a meth house. I knew myself well enough to know I should get as far away from that as I could for two reasons. First, I knew the seriousness of my obvious addiction issues. But second, I was nervous about getting too close with lesbians. Intimacy with women was easier for me, because women tend to know how women feel, and I didn't have to pretend with them. I knew how badly I wanted a deep intimacy with another human being. I didn't want to contend with yet another temptation.

I knew men, on the other hand, could not be trusted! Men hurt women! A man says he loves you, only to give you a black eye the next day or shoot you up with a drug that can kill you. He can leave you pregnant and alone. Or he can choke you and spit on you. Not even Robert, as sweet as he seemed, had gained my full trust. But I knew I needed to leave, so in the next two weeks we were packed and headed back to the Midwest. I slept a lot, exhausted from the many months prior to my stay on the West Coast. I did not tell Robert about the cocaine incident at college, but I did tell him about North County and how I got the orderlies to let me out. I thought Robert would be slightly troubled about the type of woman he had picked up. But he didn't seem apprehensive about taking me to his hometown. In fact, he just smiled and gave me a wink. I thought that peculiar, but not enough for it to keep me from falling asleep and staying that way for another several hours.

When we finally arrived in Springfield, I found myself at his grandmother's home. She was a delightful lady, and I loved that she was so accepting of this stranger in her home. She proceeded to show me where the shower was so I could clean up before dinner. I found my surroundings to be settling to my soul, maybe because it reminded me a lot of the farm and how my grandma would treat guests in her house. It also made me a believer in Robert. Maybe he really was an upright guy. Maybe I would learn to love him the way I imagined

I could love someone. I certainly didn't have a clue what that looked like or felt like, but I knew I desperately wanted it. I wanted to love someone, anyone, and be loved back. I just never thought I was a worthy recipient of that love. This self-abasing theology managed to seep through every crack in my thick, self-protective armor. I sort of traced that back to my experience at St. Margaret's. No matter how many "Our Father's," "Hail Mary's," or Rosaries I completed, it did not make me good enough to be accepted into my own family. I was sure it wouldn't be enough anywhere else. I just hoped Robert would never find out any more of my secrets, because I believed that would disqualify me as girlfriend material.

We moved into a small little house, and for the first time in an awfully long time, I entertained the thought of being part of a real family. I met Robert's friends, and we got along wonderfully. Robert and I worked together, and we had Sunday dinners at his grandmother's house. Could it be that I escaped my past, and this was my reward for living through the hell and not giving up? I could and would take all my secrets to the grave if it meant belonging like this. I even briefly met his ex-wife, who seemed sweet and gracious. He later shared about his marriage, his responsibility for its demise, and his crazy love for his two daughters. I felt that his trust in me cemented our relationship even more.

It wasn't until one day when I had gone to work by myself that my world began to unravel. I returned home at the normal time to find Robert and his ex-wife in our bed, behaving like a normal married couple. I thought I swallowed my tongue. Nothing would come out! I just stood there in disbelief, utterly unable to form a clear thought in my head. How I went from zero issues to catastrophic problems in a split second, I'll never know. My dreams of a happily-ever-after were squashed like an unsuspecting bug on a bustling city sidewalk. This was just the type of lifestyle I thought I was leaving behind. What happened to the promise I made to myself to turn over a new leaf, find a decent guy, and have the life I had always envisioned? I thought I had truly found it.

Before I had time to process the event unfolding before my eyes, Robert stopped long enough to tell me to join them. His ex-wife maintained her sweet persona. She echoed his desire with a wink and a summons to come join them. Why didn't I just give them both a piece of my mind and storm out? Instead, what came creeping into the recesses of my mind was a whisper: "Once a whore, always a whore." In order to acquiesce to Robert's demands, lest I face his fist, I began to say to myself, "Willie doesn't exist. Willie doesn't exist." It was the only way I could endure what was about to take place.

12

More Angelic Assistance

I stuffed down every emotion I had and became like a marionette in the hands of some unseen force. I simply couldn't let myself feel the betrayal and rejection. I don't know much about how the human psyche works, but I can tell you that something inside me just accepted what had been spoken over me. I felt I would never be able to escape from it. A piece of me—if not all of me—became absolute in my indifference to people and to life. I would be all things to all people, no matter how perverse. The real Willie was lost.

Several months later, one of Robert's friends told me of a job he thought I should apply for—he said the money was crazy good, and I would for sure get the job. When he said I could make several hundred dollars a day in cash, it was a no-brainer. The name of the place was Scorpios, but I still didn't know what type of establishment it was. I was naive, but I also didn't care. I saw dollar signs and a chance to get away. When I mentioned to Robert that I was going to apply, he just smiled. Later I found out that Robert was the one who got me the job. The owner was a friend of his.

I drove to the outskirts of Springfield to what appeared to be an oversized trailer. I stepped inside and observed several ladies milling around, an older woman seated at a desk inside the door, and strange lighting. I saw a man and woman head down a hallway and into a room. I spoke to a genuinely nice lady named Debbie, who, when I asked for an application, gave an amused chuckle. She said, "He will be right with you." I must have looked as confused as a cat on a leash.

Debbie walked me back into one of the many rooms. Inside was what looked like a massage table, a smaller table with a lamp and candle on it, and a coat rack. Debbie said the owner, Rick, would be there soon. She told me to take off my clothes, lie down, and get comfortable. I said, "Take off my clothes?" She laughed and said, "Yup. He's got to see the goods!" I wasn't about to show my fear, but when she asked me my age and I answered,

More Angelic Assistance

I saw hers. Barely keeping my nerves at bay, I stripped down and sat on the cold table. I couldn't bring myself to lie down. Rick walked in and gazed at me as if I were a raw steak, and he was determining how he wanted me prepared. A man of very few words, he finally spoke. He warned, "We make lots of money here. But I only hire girls eighteen or over. If you are going to stay, you better be at least eighteen. You are eighteen, aren't you, Angel?" His voice was disturbing, but I assured him that I was eighteen. I chose to keep the name he had given me.

There it was again, that declaration inside my head: "Once a whore, always a whore!" But for some twisted reason, being called "Angel" somehow made me feel better about my new career. Besides, I was only going to do it long enough to stash away a significant amount of cash. Then I would bolt. I knew Debbie had told Rick my true age, but the unspoken threat was enough to keep me quiet. My picture was taken, and I was given an identification card that would help keep my secret safe. Debbie must have realized how ignorant I truly was because she took pity on me and filled me in on all the massage parlor jargon. The typical "John" paid twenty-five dollars to be massaged with his clothes off. I would be "fully" (really, scantily) clothed. There was a "tip jar" that made all the exchanges "legal." At least that is what I was told. I was in unfamiliar territory, so whether it was legal or not I haven't a clue. My first night I did not waste any time. I made five hundred dollars. clearly we were performing more than just massages.

I should have been more clever, but I showed Robert what I had made. His pupils turned to dollar signs. He became greedy and wanted more and more material things with the money I had earned. It wasn't long before he had taken all the money I had brought home and bought his first Harley motorcycle. Now I had to do more to make more, so I could save enough to leave. It was vicious and exhausting.

I got extremely sick after several months. I had contracted a sexually transmitted disease. We were careful at work, but I knew Robert was being regularly promiscuous. It was clear I got it from him. He disgusted me. I made the mistake of sharing my feelings of revulsion. I went back to work the next night with a fat lip and a black eye. Debbie and the girls hovered over me like a mom and several big sisters. As twisted as it sounds, I would have stayed there because of the solidarity of all the girls had it not been for Tony.

Tony was the next angel God sent. Tony was kind, yet relentless in his charge to save me from myself. His methods, though undeniably effective, may give some readers great pause. But if he had not come into Scorpios that night, I am almost certain the next black eye, broken jaw, or loose tooth Robert inflicted would have been his last. That same uncontrollable rage that almost took the life of my own sister was still alive deep inside me. I wasn't sure at what point I would snap, but I knew at some point all the powers of hell would break loose and target yet another abuser.

Up until this point, most of my relationships with men were in one way or another abusive, and I was still only a teenager. I realized later that Tony hadn't been sent just to rescue me from the situation with Robert. He had been on a mission from God to start the redemptive process in my soul—one that would take almost four decades. God knew I would need proof that I wasn't just a dead woman walking. He also knew that control was my "god" and that I had turned off the physical response "switch" in my body. I vowed to never experience sexual pleasure while with a man. My chances of ever having real sexual intimacy with a husband one day were less than zero percent. That ship had sailed a long time ago, and I shredded the sails on purpose to cope with all the sordid and immoral exploits that made up the fabric of my life so far. Who would want someone as base as myself? I was damaged goods. A hideous display of depravity. I was so emotionally unhealthy that not one good thing about me would absorb into my heart and mind. I was ready to dump Robert, live with one of the girls, and maybe eventually work my way up to taking over the mother-hen duties, like Debbie. Robert had taken all my money (thousands of dollars) and left me with a sexually transmitted disease. I was drowning. In this lowest of lows. I said a three-word prayer, "God, please help!" That is when my angel Tony appeared on the scene.

It was an unusually slow weekend night, but I still had several hundred dollars in my stash box. We had hoped for more business so we could have more cash with which to escape. Debbie and a couple of the other girls were going to help get me out of there and on a plane to anywhere but Springfield. Debbie saw what my relationship with Robert and my job were doing to me. I may have come in looking like an angel, but I was certainly transforming into something else. But the slow weekend made me hesitate about leaving. After weighing all my options, I had resigned myself to working as a prostitute.

Just as I made that decision, in walked this short, plump man with a sweet smile. He was just as jolly as he was round. I got a case of the giggles (so did a few of the other girls), mainly because he looked like someone who might be going into Chuck E. Cheese for some innocent fun with his grandkids. He wasn't too old. He looked decent and very well dressed—casual, but classy. As he talked with Debbie, all ten of us girls got into formation so he could take his pick. But before he even turned around and looked at us, he told Debbie he wanted Angel.

I had never seen this man before—not on the streets of the town and certainly not in here. Debbie hadn't even called us out by name. When he finally did look up, my eyes met his, and suddenly I felt embarrassed, intimidated, and somehow fearful. Had one of my customers sent him my way? No. He told Debbie he was just passing through town. It was his eyes. They were loving and frightening at the same time. There was kindness and gentleness behind them. But also, a force I couldn't comprehend. He looked at me as though he knew me, and I didn't like how I was feeling. I also didn't like the fact that I was feeling anything at all. But I quickly took control of the situation and became unusually brazen, overplaying my part. I had to nip this in the bud—and fast. He was obviously unfamiliar with any establishment of this sort. He even blushed at the sight of the other women, who were also wearing almost nothing. He wasn't lusting. He was embarrassed for the girls and their lack of modesty. What kind of creature was this? Was this a Jekyll and Hyde kind of situation? My mind was reeling. How would I manage this "whorehouse virgin" (if he really was one)? He opened the door for me and gently shut it behind us. It was time to dig deep, because it was going to be like attempting to seduce my grandpa. What happened next, I will never be able to explain sufficiently, and it wasn't until after my salvation in 1982 that I understood God had sent Tony, His angel, to help pull me out of the darkness.

Once in the room, I began my usual cathouse banter. Tony, as sweetly and politely as I have ever been spoken to, said, "There won't be any need for that, Willie." He used my real name!!! How did he know my name? I was unquestionably shaken by such an invasion of my privacy, but I responded, "The name's Angel." Tony said, "All right, Angel, would you mind lying down?" This was not the typical order of things, but it was his dime and easy money for me. I offered, "I can slip these panties off in no time and make your experience that much more pleasurable." That would cost twenty-five dollars more. But Tony said that would not be necessary. He would prefer I stay fully dressed. What kind of kinky act did this guy have up his sleeve anyway?

I wasn't prepared for this seemingly purpose-driven appointment. Part of me was relieved I didn't have to strip down so another man could look at me like I was some holiday banquet spread. The other part was still freaked out by his familiarity with me. He continued

More Angelic Assistance

talking as though it was just another day and we were sharing sweet tea on my granny's porch. He told me about his day and asked me about mine. I wanted to be harsh and tell him to "pee or get off the pot!" Time was money, and I wasn't going to score here. But those eyes. They were so soft and kind, yet convicting. I found myself unable to speak or even look away from them. He stood beside me as I lay on my back. He continued to share what was on his mind, until his hands came out of his pockets and made their way toward my body. Why was I so disturbed? I had been in countless similar situations in this place, but with dirty, disgusting men doing even dirtier, disgusting acts. Tony never laid a finger on me! He simply put his hands over the top of my body and began talking, but not to me. Quietly and peacefully, he whispered something. At that moment, my body responded in a way I was unable to control. This man elicited sensations I tried so hard to suppress. I had no control over what was happening to me and I was terrified and angry. Allowing my body to physically respond to anyone was against every "control" rule I had made for myself. Control was my god! I can't tell you how long I laid there, but when I opened my eyes, Tony was gone. I was up off that table in less than a second and out the door. He wasn't anywhere—not in the hallway, and no one had seen him leave either.

At that moment, I fell apart. I ran to tell Debbie I was quitting! I wanted out! She could tell Rick in the morning. I was sobbing and literally freaking out. Debbie begged me to calm down. She said she would call Rick and have him come over (he was building a nightclub and restaurant next door) so I could tell him what happened, but I didn't even know myself, so how was I supposed to explain it? By that point, I was shaking and pacing like a caged animal, panicked and desperately trying to escape. Where would I go? Robert would not be happy that his money supply was about to dry up. I was beseeching Debbie to let me leave. She must have known something I didn't, because she looked panicked too (but I'm guessing for different reasons).

Rick showed up around the same time Robert did, and there was a conversation between the two of them. But before I knew it, Robert was told to wait outside. Rick took me to a small office and tried to calm me down. Rick told me he understood and would not make me stay. I thought for a second that I misjudged him in the beginning. Maybe he was really a decent guy. But once I was calmer and my breathing had slowed to a reasonable pace, he began to explain further. It was clear I was not leaving the "business." Rick went on: "I'll give you a job at The Loft (his nightclub) next door as a 'hostess.' Just make all my guests feel welcome, and you will be fine. Oh, and by the way, Robert will see to it that you get to work." Up until that point, I didn't know they knew each other. But clearly there was a connection that I assume was a business arrangement that benefited them both. I was (so I was told) one of the most profitable prostitutes Rick employed, and he had no intention of losing me. I guess he thought I was just young and naive enough to go along with it, but I wanted to get as far away as I could. One way or another, I was leaving.

That night after I got home, Robert echoed the words I heard the night my dad dragged me up the stairs. Robert asked, "So, you are a whore?" As if he didn't know where the five hundred dollars a night came from! I said, "What kind of a fool doesn't know what his woman is doing every night?" He proceeded to slap me across the face multiple times. Then he punched me in the stomach until I fell to the ground. I didn't speak or resist. As the beating continued, I just focused on how I was going to escape. That somehow it made it bearable. Afterward, I was most upset about the loose teeth.

I was dropped off at The Loft the next night. I dressed to be "eye candy." If they wanted to touch, I wasn't to resist. Still, it was better than my job at Scorpios. I was in a great mood because I planned to escape the very next day. I made a lot of money that night in tips from wealthy drunk men. I played them like old rusty fiddles.

Mender of the Broken

I was grateful I had enough cash to make it to wherever I was going, even though I had no idea where that would be. The next night I dressed for work. Because Robert had the only vehicle and he was taking me to work, he believed he had me right where he wanted me—totally dependent on him. What he didn't know was that although he and Rick had arranged for Debbie to bring me home, she was taking me to the airport instead. She was willing to pay the price for betraying them. Robert had decided to go dancing that night, so he would be out late. He would also be inebriated and less likely to wonder where I was. He never really considered that I might use the brain God gave me to find a way out! Later that night, I said my good-byes to Debbie and thanked her for her bravery. I didn't care where the flight took me that night. I only knew I needed to find one that was leaving immediately in case Robert and Rick came looking for me.

God is such an amazing Father, and as I look back now, I feel an overwhelming sense of gratitude to Him for being there with me, even though I never acknowledged His involvement in my life. Even though we have agency to live our lives the way we choose, God is still there making our mistakes work out for His glory. If we love God and are called according to His purpose, it will also ultimately work together for our good![18] We are never too soiled to be made clean again. No matter what, we can never be disqualified from being loved by God and from having a meaningful life and ultimately ministry.

I found a flight that night that was leaving in 15 minutes. Its destination was Seattle, Washington, and I knew I needed to get on that plane. I went to the ticket counter fully expecting to be told that I didn't have enough money for this last-minute ticket. But wouldn't you know it, I had just enough, with twenty-three dollars left over. So, there I was, still dressed like a Greek goddess from work, with a small box of all my belongings and a small amount of cash in my purse. I didn't even think about what I might do when I arrived in a strange city—no job, no home, and no friends or family. I didn't care. It was my chance to start again in a place where not a soul knew me. The thought of a clean slate made me feel strangely intact, and I felt this surge of hope well up in my heart.

After purchasing the ticket, I had a few minutes to wait before boarding, and suddenly fear overwhelmed me. My heart began to beat wildly, and I had a painful sensation all through my chest. I was certain others sitting close by would think I was in medical trouble and call an ambulance. I was scared out of my wits, but I had to keep it together. I expected two things to happen any moment. First, I kept thinking airport security would surround me and question why a female minor was hurrying to buy a ticket in cash. Second, I was afraid Robert or Rick (or both) would come around the corner and make me look like a troubled girl trying to run away. Any scenario other than getting on that plane and getting off the ground was unacceptable and detrimental to my plan! When they called for general boarding, I took a gasping breath that sounded like I had been underwater for a long time. I bolted from my chair and was one of the first on board. I wasn't in any frame of mind to chat with a curious seatmate. I would pretend to be asleep the whole way to Washington if I had to. Exhausted, I slept for real.

The Bible tells us that we are to show hospitality to strangers, because there are times that we encounter angels without knowing it.[19] If anyone can testify to that truth, I think I'm a good candidate. Within my first 30 minutes in Seattle, I believe I met two more angels.

I was sitting on one of the benches inside the airport, planning out my next move. It was about 2:00 a.m., and the terminal was empty, except for a few employees. I had decided I would just sleep there and find a job in the morning. It sounded reasonable and simple, and I wasn't afraid anymore. No one knew me and no one wanted to hurt me, so what did I have to worry about? I was hell-bent on making something new of my life. Again.

The bench was hard and narrow, but dawn was only a few hours away, and I was still very tired. I thought about what types of job I could get. Tomorrow I would flip through a phone book, spruce up a bit, and get myself hired.

While I was still making plans for the next day, I looked up and saw two men dressed in white from head to toe. Where they came from, I had no idea. One minute I was alone, and the next they were just there! I wasn't afraid at all, but their arrival was a bit uncanny. I looked them both over briefly and jokingly said, "What do you guys do, soak those uniforms in bleach?" They looked at each other and sheepishly laughed. Then they sat down, one on either side of me. To be honest, I somehow felt safer with them there. And unlike on the plane, I was very willing to chat. They introduced themselves as John and Scott, and I quickly made two new friends. I began to tell them my story and how I ended up in the Seattle airport in the middle of the night, carrying only a box of personal items and $23. I talked for 30 minutes straight. I wanted someone to hear it all, and I was afraid they might not be able to hang out with me for long. I just had to get it all out. These two patiently listened to me as though what I had to say was more important to them than anything else.

When I finally took a breath, they asked me if I knew anyone in Seattle. I told them no. Then they asked me if I knew anyone in Bremerton. I said, "I don't even know where Bremerton is." I then realized that their uniforms, their very white uniforms, were U.S. Navy uniforms. I mentioned I had a friend in high school who said he was going to be a doctor in the Navy someday. My friend was a considerable exaggerator and would always say he was going to do big and grandiose things with his life. Most things never panned out, so I was sure I would not find him in Bremerton.

Right then, as if on cue, they said in unison, "Great, let's go check it out." Before I knew it, I was on a ferry boat with my new friends, heading to Bremerton. It didn't really bother me that I had no real plan for the next day and that I was traveling with two male strangers on a boat. I was having the time of my life. I felt so alive.

The ferry ride was a little over an hour, and I think I talked the entire way. I was so excited to be there and away from Springfield. I was a ghost here in many ways. When I was ready, I could be anyone I wanted. In that moment, I was just happy being Willie—happy to have

More Angelic Assistance

friends who apparently wanted nothing more than to show me their beautiful state.

I felt as though I were dreaming. The cool breeze that floated so effortlessly off the top of the water gave refreshment not only to my face but also to my soul. We stood out on the bow of the ferry boat, listening to the water lap against the metal pontoons. The boat didn't go very fast, and for that I was grateful. I knew I was in the presence of goodness and kindness. I had almost forgotten what that looked or felt like.

Strangely enough, I did notice the taxi waiting when we disembarked. It was almost as if it had been called ahead of time, because without even a pause, my new sailor acquaintances politely opened the door, and in I went. We continued our conversation in the taxi. We talked about this crazy journey I was on and how I was going to make a new life in Washington, one way or another.

I remember one of them saying, "Well, I'm sure your friend will help you get started. At least you will have a place to stay for a while until you get settled." I replied, "What friend?" John smiled this lighthearted smile and said, "Mark, the friend from high school. Didn't you say your friend was in the Navy here?" After hours of talking, not only was my jaw sore, but I also wasn't sure what all I had said. I was quite sure I had told them Mark wasn't very reliable and that he liked to exaggerate for effect.

The taxi pulled into an apartment complex. You know, for a girl who is somewhat street smart, I sure was ignorant. Either that or I just chose to ignore the details—like how two strangers had earned my trust in just minutes and three hours later had delivered me to the doorstep of my friend Mark, who was indeed living in Washington and in these very apartments.

Their last words to me were, "Mark is in apartment twelve, and the door is unlocked. Just go on in." It occurred to me that they must have known Mark all along and had coordinated the whole thing after I mentioned my connection to him. I was grasping for understanding. Here's the perplexing reality: Neither Scott nor John left my side after our initial meeting at the airport. If they knew Mark, at least one of them would have had to step away to call him up, right? Doesn't that sound like the logical sequence? Nevertheless, I was grateful I had been cared for so well.

I was very tired and in desperate need of sleep. The previous 48 hours had been exhausting. I was hoping I could see my two new friends again, so I asked them to write their names on a piece of paper for me, along with the name of their ship. They obliged, smiling, and I gave them both enormous hugs and said my goodbyes. I assured them I would call the following day as soon as I had my wits about me again. They drove off, and I suddenly felt insecure. I did as they said and went to apartment twelve, opened the door, and saw Mark asleep in his studio apartment bed. He heard me come in. I had scared him, and he bolted out of his bed ready to defend himself.

The sight was simply too funny. I erupted in belly laughter. I said, "Mark, really? Boxers?" He responded quickly, "Willie, what the hell are you doing here? How did you get here? How did you know where I lived? I don't understand what is going on here." I think he was still wondering if he was dreaming. When he realized he was indeed awake, he let out an inquisitive snicker. Unsure of what had just happened, he gave me a huge hug anyway and popped open a bottle of wine. We sat on his bed, talked, drank, and laughed, and I shared the amazing night I had just had with two of his sailor brothers!

I told Mark I wanted to call the Naval station first thing in the morning, so I could talk to or leave a message with my two new friends. Mark said he didn't think a ship by that name existed, and of course, I didn't believe him. Mark dialed the number and handed me the phone. In my excitement, I must have been unclear when inquiring about the ship and my two friends. The operator reiterated the same thing Mark had claimed. That ship didn't exist! Plus, the names my friends had given were not found on the Navy roster. How could that be? I knew I hadn't been dreaming, although the entire night before was beginning to seem like one big illusion.

I recounted it all to Mark—the way the two men just happened to be at the airport and appeared right when I was trying to decide what to do. I told him about the ferry ride and the taxi that just showed up and then brought me straight to Mark's doorstep. It all seemed like something I had made up, but I knew it had all happened!

The telephone was still in my hand, even though there was only static on the other end. The Naval office had already hung up, but I was still quite bewildered. I shook it off and decided just to do what I came to Washington to do: start over. I told Mark I would find a job that day and do my best to avoid "cramping his style."

Mark was kind enough to show me around the town a little bit that morning. He said I could use his car to put in some applications at various places. I dropped him off at the Naval station, and off I went in hopes of landing a great job. I was excited about the prospect of starting fresh. It felt pure and wholesome somehow. All the past filth of my life seemed to liquefy in that single moment and drip off me like a spring shower off the leaves of trees. It was exhilarating.

I began to think about where I could find work. I was determined to get a job that day, and I didn't want to spin my wheels filling out applications at random places. I asked myself, "Willie, what do you know a lot about?" The answer came quickly. Pizza! I knew a lot about pizza and the workings of pizza restaurants, because my family owned a chain of them. As a child, I would frequent the one in my hometown, while my parents worked. I loved watching how the waitstaff interacted with the patrons. People were always laughing and enjoying themselves. I often thought I would like to be one of those waitresses someday, because they were loved and needed by those they served, and if they did a good job, there would always be a cash reward left on the table. I may have been a kid when I thought that, but I was sure the same principles still applied, so I started to look in the phone book for pizza restaurants. Then I looked up, and right across the street from where I was parked was a big sign that read "Pana's Pizza House." Big surprise, right?

I quickly looked in my rearview mirror for a once-over, checking for lingering breakfast crumbs in my teeth, and off I went. I was confident and maybe slightly cocky, but I knew I had to be. Who wants to hire a girl who is unstable, uncertain, and homeless to boot? I put on my best face, and in the door I went. I didn't stop to wonder if the restaurant was even open yet. It was only 10:00 in the morning, but the door was unlocked, so that was my cue to enter.

When I opened the door, there were several employees bustling around getting things ready for the day. Somewhere in the distance, I heard a booming yet jolly voice taking command. As it turned out, that was Mr. Pana himself. He came out from behind a wall, which I assumed was the kitchen, and saw me standing in the doorway. He said, "Well, don't just stand there. Take a seat, young lady." So, I did. It was almost as if he had been expecting me, but I knew that could not be possible. Or could it? After all the strange and unexplainable situations I'd found myself in over the past couple of years, this shouldn't have surprised me.

He introduced himself and asked how he could help. I explained that I had just gotten into town and was looking for a job. He was a very discerning man and asked, "So, on top of needing a job, you probably need a permanent place to live and adequate transportation, right?" I nodded in agreement, but not without a timid laugh to go along with my response. He asked if I had

More Angelic Assistance

any experience, and that question opened the floodgates. I began to tell him all about my parents, the restaurants they owned, and the history behind their business.

I told him of my desire to start fresh (no details were included). I'm sure I took up a lot of valuable time, but he didn't seem to care at all. He just listened intently with a smile on his face. I figured he was probably more like a dad than a boss to his employees.

Surprisingly, he gave me the job. He handed me a black apron and asked if I wanted to hang around and bus some tables, until it was time for me to pick up Mark at the Naval station. I, of course, said yes, but I also felt he had another reason for letting me stay that day. And I was right.

At around 3:00 in the afternoon, a handful of kids about my age or maybe a little older came in the door. They were obviously familiar with the place because they immediately went behind the counter, grabbed glasses, and filled them to the brim with cold soda pop. They glanced over at me, smiled, and said hello, but they quickly made their way to the back of the store, I assumed to check in with the boss or whomever they were there to see. It wasn't long before Mr. Pana came out with two of the kids. They looked oddly alike, although one was a boy and the other a girl. He introduced me to his twins,

Cathy and Curt, who were very warm and friendly, just like their dad.

For the first week on the job, Mark let me use his car, which was a real lifesaver. But I knew my time with him would come to an end soon. He had no plans to permanently house an old high school friend, and I knew he was already feeling antsy. I started to look in the papers for apartment rentals and roommate wanted ads. On the first day of my second week, I was taken off bussing duties and began to work with Cathy, learning all there was to learn about being a server at her family's pizza shop.

That evening, when it was time for me to clock out, Mr. Pana asked me to stick around for a few minutes. A wave of panic instantly rushed over me. What had I done to get fired? Or was it just a warning? I sat in one of the booths for what seemed like an eternity, but it was probably only a minute or two. Mr. Pana, Cathy, and Curt finally came out and joined me at the table. The twins had this silly grin on their faces, which made me even more confused. Without a pause, Mr. Pana simply asked if I would like to move in with Cathy and Curt, who had their own house. I could just ride in with them because we would all work the same shift. My first thought was, "Who owns a house at seventeen years old?" But I didn't care how it worked, because I was being given a rare opportunity, and I wasn't about to pass it up. I really liked the twins. We had become instant friends during that first week, and I was excited about the fact that I was going to have a home, a great job, and the chance to be part of a real family. The idea that I could start over was not just a dream anymore. It had been realized largely because of two kind, tenacious, and blazingly white angels who had come to my rescue at the airport.

Life was good, and I was happy for a while. I worked full time at Pana's and enjoyed living with Cathy and Curt, who had quite the setup. They were exceptionally good at playing the straight and narrow, but these two also loved their social gatherings. I had not yet learned the secret to setting boundaries for myself, so I generally found myself in the middle of every shindig thrown at their home. In my heart, I wanted a clean break from the "old" Willie, but temptation was hard to resist. I met several new friends through the twins, but rule number one was that I was to be loyal to the Pana pair, no matter what. Their friends were to be my friends. When Cathy and Curt got tired of having certain guests around or thought they were being taken advantage of, I was expected to shun the same people, even if I personally had nothing against them. Mr. Pana's money was being misspent on just about everything, and I was expected to lie for the twins if asked.

As time went on, my relationship with Cathy and Curt became strained. I'm not exactly sure which was the final straw that broke the camel's back, but eventually, our friendship and my job at Pana's came to an end. But I found a new place to live and a new job. I loved Mr. Pana and would miss him tremendously, but I knew beyond a shadow of a doubt that blood was thicker than water. He cared about me, but I needed to move on.

I had met this much older man named Chappy. I can't recall how or where I met him, but he reminded me so much of my grandpa in Kansas. His appearance and mannerisms were remarkably similar. Somehow, we became fast friends. I was comfortable enough with him that I accepted his offer of rooming with him and a new job carrying large panes of glass throughout Washington state. I got to see so much of that beautiful part of the country, with its lush green scenery and mile after mile of the most stunning bodies of water I had ever seen. It was picturesque.

I loved those drives and views. I believe Chappy was also sent by God. Angel? Someday I will find out I'm sure. He not only gave me a safe home, but he also showed me love, respect, and how to have a deep appreciation for

More Angelic Assistance

life. He didn't expect anything from me but a hard day's work, and that I gave him willingly.

So many decent men seemed to be strategically placed in my life to rescue me from danger. They stopped me from making even poorer choices than the ones I had already made. It was one of the deep mysteries of my life, until I put my trust in Jesus Christ. Now I see it was all God's gracious love and provision for me. That, and He wanted me to understand that not all men were jerks! ☺

Mostly, these men were placed in my life to rescue me from myself. I was like a boat without a rudder. I had no real direction. When Chappy came into my life, I still believed I was damaged goods. But Chappy didn't. He would continually argue that case. He would say, "Willie, the only one indicting you … is you. Don't you think it's time for an acquittal?" He was such a wonderful man.

I didn't know God back then, but I believe each of these incredible experiences would play a very important role in my coming to know Jesus and understanding the Father heart of God.

One night I will never forget. Chappy had dropped me off at Cathy and Curt's house to get the rest of my belongings. I assured him I could get a ride home, so, reluctantly, he left. The twins and I got into a juvenile but hurtful argument about what had led to my departure. While living with the Panas, I foolishly trusted Cathy with the awful details of my past. In this moment, in front of her brother and others, she used that knowledge against me in an abusive tirade. She basically argued, "Once a whore, always a whore." Where had I heard that before? I was truly devastated. I came to Washington to get away from that "old person" and from pitiless people. I considered her my friend, so her words stung like sleet on my face in 40-mile-an-hour wind. It was enough to send me running for reinforcements, and since I hadn't established a different way of dealing with pain yet, I reverted to my former habits. I set out with one of my more questionable friends named Terri, to try to assuage the feeling of condemnation that lay heavy on my heart.

I had called Terri to come to pick me up, and we headed to Seattle. It was a good sixty-six-mile drive from Bremerton, and it probably would have been smart to plan to stay the night there. Terri wanted to show me the city. In actuality, she simply wanted me to see the inside of as many bars as possible. Seven hours later, I would have another angelic visitation, but this time a familiar face from the past.

I remember, that night the hot buttered rums flowing endlessly, and after a few hours, I knew if we didn't leave Seattle soon, we would be in trouble. Where we ended up that night depended on my ability to get us out of there. I grabbed Terri by the arm and told her it was time to end the party. We somehow (I know now it was by the grace of God) found her car, and although neither of us was in any condition to drive, I was the only choice. Once I put Terri in the car, she went comatose. I saw signs for Bremerton, and though I was terrified, I tried to make out which of the roads in my double vision was the right road.

I crossed my fingers and went for it. It was approximately 3:00 in the morning, and I guess I was driving too fast for that gear, because suddenly, I heard a boom! Then the car came to a quick stop on the highway. I looked around and only saw darkness. There were no signs telling me where I was, and I was having a hard enough time simply focusing on the dashboard. I sat there for a while until headlights appeared in my rear-view mirror. Whoever it was pulled in directly behind us, and I instantly began to panic.

If it was the police, I would be in serious trouble for so many reasons. I didn't know Terri well enough to know if this was even her car. But if not, the police, who

I was about to encounter? My mind was racing, and I immediately locked the doors and just waited.

I watched someone get out of the driver's side and make his way to my window. I was afraid to look, but when I heard a gentle tap on the window, I reigned in all the fear welling up inside me and turned to see who was standing there. Once I looked up, the first thing I felt was paralyzing fear. Then an unexplainable calm. I wasn't sure if all the alcohol was causing hallucinations, so I did a double take. When I shook off the initial shock, I realized they were those same kind eyes that met mine that fateful night at Scorpios. It was Tony! How was this possible? It was the middle of the night, in the middle of nowhere, in a different state. I was in a very precarious situation, but I needed help. And who knew who might come along if I didn't accept his help. So I rolled down my window just enough to speak, but not enough for an arm to reach in and unlock the door. I don't remember saying anything except that my friend was passed out and I had no idea where I was or where home was. He spoke to me in the most compelling way. I don't know how else to explain it. He was authoritatively kind and gentle. He told me to unlock the passenger side door so he could carry Terri to his car. I obeyed, and then I watched as he carefully picked her up. He looked at her with such compassion, as though she were his own daughter and he was anguished over her situation. Then he returned for me. I honestly don't remember unlocking my door, but he opened it and offered me his hand. We walked in silence to his car, and I got in the front next to Terri and Tony. I reiterated that I was utterly lost and had no idea how to get home. I wanted so badly to ask him to confirm that he was the same man from that night in Missouri, but in my innermost being, I knew he was. I knew he had been there the night my fortified wall had come crashing down. The control I thought I had was just an illusion. I remained quiet.

About forty-five minutes later, we pulled into a very long dirt driveway that led us to Chappy's trailer door. I was so relieved to see it that I failed to even consider how Tony had found it. I quickly got out of the car and opened the door. This man, who now had rescued me twice, laid Terri on the couch. In a matter of seconds, I covered her with the blanket that was folded up on the back of the couch, and I turned to thank him. But he was nowhere to be found. I thought maybe he was walking back to his car, but I looked out the door and there was no car. No car, no taillights, no sign that he was ever there. I stood looking around the trailer, wondering for a moment if this was all just a dream and I would soon wake up with a bad hangover. But it wasn't a dream. The next day Chappy's dog woke me up. Terri was already gone. Chappy must have taken her home. We never spoke about that night.

I knew I could have continued working with him, and living in his trailer, but we both knew it was time for me to start a life of my own. Chappy didn't argue, he simply promised he would always be there to help if I needed him.

Come Monday, I was excited about the adventure and future that awaited me. Chappy lent me his truck that evening, and I dressed in one of only two outfits I owned (a skirt, a blouse, and my favorite go-go boots) to search for a job. It was a new day, and although my mind and heart were filled with questions about my mysterious angel of mercy, I was grateful to be alive. I was hopeful and ready to begin again. How many do-overs can one person get? Jesus instructed the disciples to forgive again and again. How many times? Seventy times seven! A day![20] I am so grateful my God is a forgiving God.

After all the help and protection I had received, I knew something or someone powerful was watching over me. I wouldn't know *how true* that really was until sometime later.

I will always believe in and be grateful for each angel God so lovingly positioned at each critical crossroad in my life.

13

CHOICES AND CONSEQUENCES

I set off to look for a job in Chappy's truck, but true to my nature, I was drawn to the crowd in town. I was sure to get plenty of attention walking along the sidewalk in my short skirt, tight white shirt, and blue go-go boots. I headed toward a strip of nightclubs that lay tucked away beneath a scenic backdrop of Mt. Rainier. It felt like I was being called to participate in the pleasure of it all. Maybe I could enjoy part of the evening before I succumbed to a 9:00 to 5:00 job. I really was ready to start over, again! But that didn't mean I couldn't also have some fun.

I had already had so many personal do-overs. But I honestly believed every "new leaf" would be the one that would magically turn things around for me. I believed it, I wanted it more than anything, and I was going to do everything in my power to prove to myself I was worthy of a good life and that I had something good to offer another human being. But so far, each "new leaf" turned out to be just another old sprig off a dead tree. I could change on the outside like a chameleon, but inside—in my heart and soul—I was still drowning in that black, icky abyss. I would ignore it for many years still. This was the beginning of thirty-two years of marriage to four husbands.

I was eager to belong somewhere and to someone, but my choices were not wise.

Looking for love and acceptance outside the will of God is dangerous, especially for a Christian. It will surely lead to a great deal of heartache, suffering, confusion, regret, and ultimately discipline. God loves us too much not to intervene.

I can't tell you how Chappy got his truck back; I truly can't remember. I have a vague recollection that I called him and told him where he could pick it up. I never saw Chappy again.

Donny was husband number one and the father of my two children. We met that night at a club in Bremerton, Washington, when I was supposed to be job hunting. He was one of the musicians in the band, and I was struck with love at first sight. After spending several days and nights with him, I believed he was "the one."

I was so infatuated with him, and I knew he had real affection for me. Whether it was love or not, I didn't know, because that wasn't something I understood. He liked me enough to have me travel on the road with his band. We returned to his parents' home in California when the tour was over. We got pregnant shortly after, and Donny's attitude changed. I don't think he wanted the responsibility of a child. Not at this point in his life anyway. I wanted to understand and be sympathetic because we were so young, and his music was his life. I think he was trying to be sympathetic towards me as well, but I could tell he was upset when he found out I was pregnant. He wouldn't say it, but when he suggested I visit Planned Parenthood, I knew the direction he was thinking.

I went to the appointment and left feeling more devalued and defeated than I did going in. They said there was no baby inside me, but just a clump of tissue, and that the "problem" could be erased just as easily as a pencil eraser erases an unwanted pencil mark. They purposely had paper and a pencil nearby. They broke down the price of the procedure right away and asked me to schedule that appointment and leave a deposit. Not a single woman in that building asked me how I was feeling or if I was scared. They failed to mention how the procedure would be done or how I would feel after the procedure was finished. I was terrified, and I knew they were wrong. That lump of tissue was a life. Not a potential life, but a life with potential. I was troubled, confused, and all alone.

I knew what was growing inside me. I was struggling to hang on to this person—this tiny human being whom no one else could bring into the world but me—and I wanted a chance to love this baby. I wanted the opportunity to love him like I was never loved. Finally, after many days of painful discussion, Donny suggested that maybe it was time for me to return to my family in Missouri. I knew that was not an option. Where would I go? I knew no one else in California, and because I was still so crippled with self-doubt, I felt I had no other option. When the procedure was about to begin, I began to weep and yelled at the doctor to STOP! He was clearly angry and told his nurse to lay over the top of my body to keep me still. I was terrified! He spoke sharply to me and said if I moved, irreparable damage could occur and make it impossible for me to have children in the future.

I wept the entire time. My first child died on April 9, 1979. It was one of the saddest days of my life!

Just two months after destroying one life, I was pregnant with another. I told Donny; I would not endure another abortion.

It was a very fearful and difficult time for so many reasons. Four months into my pregnancy, Donny abandoned me to pursue other female interests, when he wasn't playing with his band in the nightclubs. I knew he was simply scared, but it didn't lesson the feeling of rejection a single ounce. I moved in with his sister while Donny continued living at his mom's.

When I was almost six months pregnant, he called and asked me to meet him on the road, so we could try to work things out. I was so hopeful. We spent the next month getting to know one another again. The first time our son kicked, hands on my swollen belly, we cried together and together looked forward to the future. We talked names and how we would raise him. We laughed and cried as we shared our hopes and dreams with one another. But on the return home, he became extremely sick. Among other things, Donny's sight was diminishing, and we didn't know why.

We headed to an emergency room in San Diego where we were both examined by the doctors.

My baby was healthy, but I was not. I was critically stressed, and it wasn't about to get better. The diagnosis for Donny was grim. The father of my child was now dying of cancer. All our dreams shattered in an instant! Three months into his chemotherapy, we welcomed a baby boy.

After months and months of grueling chemotherapy, Donny went into remission and I became pregnant for the third time. This time we had a little girl. We got married. Regrettably, when she was less than two years old, we divorced. The stress of it all proved to be too challenging for both of us.

Divorce is so difficult for everyone, and especially for the children involved. To this day, my grown children will attest to that truth. I had always hoped I would find true love, have children, raise them in the same house all their lives, share their joys and their pains, see them off to college, and then grow old with my husband as we welcomed grandchildren and great-grandchildren. That was my dream.

At this point in my life, all my dreams had been so shattered that I never dared to dream like that again.

I had two precious babies to consider now. I was a single parent, yet the Lord knew my heart and my desire to be a good mother. In His great mercy, He delivered me completely of the desire for drugs.

It was while I was married to Donny that I met Jesus.

After my first divorce, I felt brushed aside. I stayed in San Diego with my two small children and lived in a small apartment on government assistance. I was raising them basically alone. While Donny flaunted his leggy, beautiful blonde girlfriend each time he came to pick up the children for visits, I was a young, tired mother who believed I would never be good enough to hold on to a man. Just another arrow from the enemy meant to pierce my self-confidence.

Turns out, this beautiful blonde was a wonderful, nurturing stepmom. My kids loved her and so did I. I thanked the Lord for her every day!

Life was difficult for a single mom on welfare. I wasn't accustomed to being alone, and I worried about my children growing up without a father figure in the home. Let me say right now; neither being lonely nor wanting a father figure around is a good reason to go looking for "love." Being desperate for connection instead of trusting God to provide what you need might end you up on a road that leads to even more heartache. It did for me.

During this vulnerable time in my life, Ben and his daughter Ruth came into the picture. She was four years old at the time, and he was almost twenty years my senior. I was still a new Christian, and he was a seasoned believer who quoted Scripture, was faithful in church, read his Bible, sang in the choir, and said all the honorable things. He said he believed the Lord put his apartment above mine in our apartment complex because I was meant to be with him. Why wouldn't I believe him? After all, he claimed to have this personal relationship with God, and I was alone and lonely and a baby Christian. Ben wanted to mentor and disciple me. After only five months, he asked me to marry him and I said yes. I just knew this time life was going to be beautiful, because God would be at the center of our relationship.

Alarm bells should have been blaring during the two months prior to the wedding. I was trying hard to be virtuous. I knew I was forgiven of my past and wanted to please God with the rest of my life. I thought I was safe, and Ben would be the one to help me become the woman of God I had envisioned. Except for the multitude of apologies and asking to be forgiven, the acts he wanted me to perform (pre-wedding) took me back to my days at Scorpios. During this time, I began to realize I may have made another profoundly serious mistake. By now, Ben was planning our wedding, and I was trying to figure out how to stop it from happening. I know he sensed my trepidation, so he carefully solicited our church friends to help me "see the light." They, of course, did not know the perversion that was being asked of me. Nor did they know how he took his anger out on me and on my young son. He told them I was worried about the age difference.

Everyone believed he was this godly man God had ordained to be my husband except one person, Cathy, the woman who led me to the Lord. She was not only opposed but declined to attend the ceremony. She told me Ben was not the husband God had chosen for me. When I told Ben what Cathy had said, thinking he too might want to prayerfully reconsider, he became angry and told me that Satan can use even the most well-meaning people to try and stop His plans. Ben said I was his Gomer and he was my Hosea. But he was no Hosea.

I wanted to go to the pastor of our church and tell him what really went on behind closed doors. But I was too afraid, and we did get married. Our married years were turbulent. He was careful to be the "church man" when others were watching, but like in my childhood, there was a terrible spirit permeating our home. We were married for ten years, and then we divorced. It was only by the grace of God that I was able to leave.

Sadly, my stepdaughter, Ruth, was not permitted to live with me as I had hoped. I was denied visits with her unless I reconsidered the divorce and came home. Since that was not an option for me, Ruth and I didn't reconnect for many years. This was difficult for me and her stepbrother and sister.

Years later, I heard from a friend in California that Ben had genuinely repented and took responsibility for the demise of our marriage. I was told he made a fresh start with a wonderful woman in his church, who he remained married to until his death. Although I had moved away, Ruth stayed and enjoyed many wonderful years with her dad. I was grateful to a very merciful God who loves us and never gives up on us. God Is Healer!

Dave was husband number three. Dave, me, and my two children left California for Oklahoma where he had family. Leaving California meant a fresh start. This was the one relationship in which I never experienced any abuse. Dave and I were married for nine years, and together we ran a successful business and had many wonderful friends. I loved his family so very much, and I knew how much they loved me.

I take full responsibility for the demise of this relationship. One day I hope to share my deep regret with Dave face-to-face. He did not deserve that kind of treatment.

Although I had grown and overcome so many adversities, I was still broken in so many ways. The devil knew exactly when and how to find me and attack me. I was restless in the relationship. Being an Alpha female and used to strong men (albeit abusive men), Dave's quiet, passive personality proved more challenging for me. Restless, I wanted a fight. I wanted to know if I mattered. I wanted to feel something passionate, something fiery in the relationship. That never materialized. These struggles, along with Charles (husband number four), are what Satan used to end my friendship and marriage with Dave.

After three failed marriages, it became nearly impossible for me to have healthy relationships of any kind. Even though Dave really loved me and was committed to helping me on so many levels, I could not reciprocate. He was the only one of the four who did not cause serious physical or mental harm to me. Instead, I hurt him. The cycle of dysfunction in my life seemed endless. Ultimately, my history of unhealthy relationships made it nearly impossible to understand or fully accept

God as a Father and Friend, Jesus as Savior, and the Holy Spirit as Comforter.

I think because I was raised to devalue myself, I did not seek help to change that narrative. I didn't know had badly I was broken. I just knew I was. I would cling to whatever "normalcy" was present and bury the other ugly aspects in that same deep cistern of my soul. I didn't know what it was like to be loved or wanted or protected. I had not learned love from my own father. I only knew how to detest myself and distrust men.

I was already so emotionally damaged by this time, that the painful experiences from my first, second, and third marriage were enough to set the stage for Satan to attempt to destroy me altogether.

I married husband number four six months after leaving Dave. Charles and I were married for seven years, and then he died. This relationship is by far the most difficult for me to explain. I would like to believe that he could have turned things around if he would have simply believed in the power of the cross for himself, truly repented, and made things right with those he did so much damage to. After all, doesn't Jesus say that he wishes none would perish? So, in my heart I had to believe this scripture included Charles, even though I didn't want it to. The damage was extensive! But who was I to condemn him? Some say that he was too deep in Satan's camp to be one of the redeemed. But even though I despised what he had done, I believe that there is no sin, no matter how grievous, that is unforgiveable. That is how powerful the cross is. How thankful I am because there were some who thought I was just as unredeemable.

Charles lived a childhood story, that in many ways, was more gruesome than my own. So, my heart resonated with that person. I understood his brokenness and did not want to minimize the pain he suffered, or the effects of a childhood gone wrong. Sadly, he used the compassion I had for him to twist and bend my mind in ways that has taken me over a decade to recover from.

Somehow, he believed he was helping others by using his knowledge and skill to manipulate and alter another person's mind and will. He was able to trigger emotions that caused others to be vulnerable and open to suggestion. I know now that he did this for his own purpose and agenda. Having this power over another human being gave him purpose. But as it was happening to me and other friends I knew, we were convinced that it was for our own good.

The depraved side of this man was calculating and intentional. He tore me down intellectually and emotionally with hours and hours of mental manipulation, better known as gaslighting. **(See the Resource and Information page for further explanation.)**

Mental suffering is different from other forms of abuse. When your mind is sick, it affects your personhood—the very essence of who you are. Charles was making my mind sick on purpose.

This abuse proved much harder to recover from. He crossed serious moral and ethical lines and wounded other tender souls besides mine. He could persuade vulnerable men and women that his methods provided the only true road to recovery. With his claims to be a licensed therapist, he offered documents that seemed to prove it. If in fact this was true, it would make his abuse that much more heinous!

Charles came on the scene while I was still married to Dave. Dave and I were running a successful business together when Charles showed up. He came in almost every day. He watched and took notes. He picked up on my lack of contentment in the marriage. He used that to reel me in. Charles was on staff at a church in our town and was soon counseling Dave and me. At first, I believed Charles was going to fix us. He eventually convinced me that I married Dave for all the wrong reasons, and it was God's will that I should leave him. He said I should have never settled for less than what God wanted for me. Charles also reminded me of my previous failed marriages and that this marriage to Dave was no different. He asked me if the Lord gave me His blessing to marry any one of the three husbands, and I had to admit that I never asked God. I just "felt" marrying Dave was going to be good for me and the kids because Dave was kind and his family amazing. Remember, I had just come out of a damaging relationship with Ben. Dave stood up to Ben at one point and told him to leave me alone.

I was so conflicted. It was true, I needed more from Dave emotionally, but I was scared. Part of me wanted him to swoop in and fight for me, to fight for us. I needed him to safeguard me from Charles' grip over me. I was so confused, and I did not want another divorce "under my belt." I did not want to hurt Dave or his family either. During the one-on-one sessions, Charles was able to create in my heart deep resentment and discontent towards Dave. Years later I understood that this was his plan all along. Looking back, it was so sinister.

Dave was a wonderful person. He was, however, extremely passive, and he never challenged me, even when I disrespected him and our marriage covenant. I cared for him very much, but I wasn't capable of real intimacy. It wasn't anything I had ever known or experienced. I was sick in my heart and so terribly broken that nothing Dave could have done would have healed the wounds only God could heal.

All this personal information came out in counseling meetings with Charles, and he was quick to capitalize on it. Charles made his move. He began to spend more and more time counseling me alone, and those sessions consisted of some very intense conversations. He knew enough about psychology to bypass the ego and super-ego and go straight for the Id. He created intrigue and mystery in my mind, and as a result, I was less and less content at home with Dave.

I ended up leaving Dave and marrying Charles before I understood the darkness I was about to encounter. Ironically, I had Dave's approval and blessing. This would have never been the case if Charles had not spent hours with Dave doing the same mind alteration he did to me. Charles made Dave believe that I would never be healed in my current environment. Whatever his counselling entailed, it drastically changed the way Dave saw me. Charles got the ball rolling, and his plan progressed at full speed.

Charles was a predator, although I didn't understand that completely until years after his death and after excruciating months of legitimate therapy. He knew exactly what he was doing and where I was the weakest and most vulnerable. He took advantage of my broken spirit and a lifetime of unresolved pain. He knew I struggled with my own sexual aversions and my deep-seated need to be free from my past. The strongholds in my heart and mind were fortified with doubt, fear, hopelessness, and a whopping dose of shame.

Week after week, he wore me down with hours of psychotherapy. He really made me believe he was the answer, sent by God to bring about healing in my mind, body, and spirit. If I didn't acquiesce to his demands, there would be repercussions. These repercussions included hours of gaslighting until I was so totally susceptible that I would agree to whatever suggestion was presented. This made my life even more emotionally stressful, which added to my insecurity. That was also his plan.

I didn't comprehend for a long time just how twisted he was. He had a blueprint right from the start. He would build me up and then tear me down in order to keep me confused, insecure, and unsure of my own thoughts. He used my flaws and limitations against me. He claimed to restore rape victims to sound persons again. He said he had helped many women with stories like mine. Maybe he really believed this about himself because he had to make some sense of his own abuse.

For years, he used me to fulfill his own sexual fantasies. He said regression therapy (reliving my past sexual exploits, but this time with the ability and power to say "no") would cure me and that if I ever wanted to truly be free, I needed to cooperate with the process. If I ever hesitated, he would say I would be broken forever, and my children would be just as broken because of me. So, I continued to follow his course.

He would take me to strip clubs or massage parlors, looking for women to "help." Really, he just wanted to watch his wife seduce another woman and be part of the whole sick scene. Sadly, I submitted. Playing whatever part he wanted me to play made my life easier with him. I certainly was not a stranger to this scene. **"Once a whore, always a whore, Willie."** I just thought by now that was all I was good for. Saying "no" was not an option.

At this point, I seriously considered ending my life.

I remember a long night of gaslighting. I was so tired of the mental abuse. I couldn't take any more. I remember screaming at Charles at the top of my lungs for him to stop! I begged him to leave me alone. I was fighting for my sanity but losing the battle. I ran to our bedroom and into the closet. I knew there was a loaded pistol on the top shelf. My hands trembled as I slowly pointed it to my head. I began to cry as I slid to the floor, wanting to go through with it just to escape the madness.

Something inside me knew how grieved the Lord was, but I was so far from the Holy Spirit that I could not hear His voice any more. I was so desperate to be liberated from this prison and the chains that had shackled me all my life. I would have done just about anything to find a cure for the sickness that went all the way to the core of my being. Even if it was death. I thought about my children, put the gun on the floor and wept.

How does a person treat you this way and still declare their undying love for you? Even though I saw glimpses of what I thought was love, months of therapy after his death helped me understand something vastly different. God is love. True love. If we say we love people and then lead them into sin or compromise, that is not love. If we say we love people and then manipulate them to serve ourselves, that is not love. If we say we love people and yet we are willing to inflict needless pain, that is not love.

"Love is patient, love is kind. It does not envy, it does not boast, it is not proud. It is not rude, it is not self-seeking, it is not easily angered, it keeps no record of wrongs. Love does not delight in evil but rejoices with the truth. It always protects, always trusts, always hopes, always perseveres. Love never fails."[21]

How could something so sinister be invisible to my heart? I had fallen for so many of Satan's lies. He is the father of lies and deception. How desperately we need to know Jesus and be in relationship with Him continually. To fully remain in Him and in His love is the only way to be free!

There were periods of time where we were too busy traveling or building businesses to play these twisted games of his, but he always tried to make me feel broken and in need of his "therapy." In his narrative, he was the bridge to hope. He was the anointed one sent by God. He was the physician who would heal. These were his claims, and he was convincing.

The only real reprieve from him I experienced was a few years into our marriage. A lump had formed on my neck, and it turned out to be stage four Metastatic Squamous Cell Carcinoma. It had spread into my lymph system. I underwent a radical dissection of my neck and endured months of radiation to my head and neck. After about a week of treatment, I was unable to eat, and a feeding tube was placed in my stomach. Within six months I had lost seventy-five pounds. I was an extremely sick woman, and because of that, Charles left me alone. During this time, I was relieved and even grateful that I had cancer.

Five years after my diagnosis, the cancer was in full remission! Prior to that, I was told I would probably die, but that if I made it through the initial surgery, I would never speak again, my shoulder would not function, and my face would resemble someone with severe Bell's Palsy. They did have to remove some of my tongue, but I woke up from surgery determined to make it out of this victorious!

The Lord was (and is) so good. I was talking within hours after coming out of anesthesia—not very well, but still talking. The doctors were amazed! The devil would try several more times to bring me to my demise, but he would be unsuccessful each time. Satan was not having any success trying to kill my body, so he focused more on destroying my mind.

While I was recovering from treatment at home, Charles was busy procuring a company out of Europe. Charles' business savvy combined with the technology of this company proved to be a legitimate partnership. All parties chose to continue the relationship in the United States. It was a successful motorcycle company that owned several small planes.

One fateful Saturday, Charles, along with two other top executives in the company were to take a newly acquired plane to Montana for an investors' meeting. It would be a one-day trip. Charles and I had fought the night before, so I declined to go. The plane never made it back. It crashed, and all three executives perished. Charles was the pilot. Although he was a seasoned pilot, he hadn't flown this particular plane much before.

As tragic as that was, I was finally able to start healing after Charles died. He could no longer torment me. I will always feel some responsibility for the death of the other two men in the plane. I suppose I felt this way because Charles knew on his return that I was going to leave him, and in his mind that was not an option. Was his focus on how to keep me and not on the critical fuel level in the plane? Did knowing I would leave him unless he came clean about the hundreds of thousands of dollars he embezzled from investors prove too much for him to bear? If I had tried to smooth things over, would the other two men still be alive? I will never know.

I loved the other families. I watched their wives and children grieve the loss of such love in their lives, and I grieved for them.

Now, my life was in shambles because of my decision to marry Charles. I had lost so many dear friends and family members as well as the respect of my children. I lost a thriving business I really loved. I lost an incredibly good man (Dave)—one I could have learned to have a healthy love for had we sought out legitimate counseling. I lost whatever shred I had of dignity and self-respect.

I did gain some things, however. I gained more shame and self-doubt, as if I didn't have enough already. I reached new heights of self-loathing. I gained a greater ability to detach and disconnect.

Let me be clear. I certainly am not guiltless in the demise of so much in my life. I was an unfaithful woman. I was always looking for affirmation and acceptance, even when I had it. I genuinely believe Dave loved me and tried his hardest to prove it by never judging me for the many ways I acted out. I even tried to provoke him to anger. I wanted him to neglect me or exploit me or be cruel to me so my actions would be justified. He never did.

What was the root that occupied my heart and mind so fully that I was incapable of love? I think I believed Satan's lies for so long that my entire identity was wrapped up in his valuation of me. I wrote Dave an exceptionally long apology letter, confessing the gross sin I committed against him, and I asked for his forgiveness. I never heard back from him. I do hope in his heart he did forgive me. I pray for that!

I ruined so many wonderful relationships while I was with Charles. So many! How does anyone move forward after all that? In my heart, there was so much sadness, so much brokenness, and so much regret. I still had not healed from all the ways Satan had tried to steal from me, kill me, and destroy my life.[22]

I was all alone now, except for that all too familiar feeling of unworthiness. My children were grown and gone, friends and acquaintances moved on, and I could not look to the future any more. Why would anyone want someone with this much history and substantial baggage? I became almost crippled with the humiliation of it all. I stopped living on the inside. I put on a brave face for my family and a few close friends, and I tried to find ways to be happy, but it wasn't working. I hated faking it. I needed my daddy. Not my earthly Dad, but my Daddy God. My Papa. My Jesus! I just did not know how to reach back. I knew He was there with me, wooing me, loving me. I just felt too depraved to be in His presence.

All I could see was the damage done. I ruined many marriages—my own and others. I took the life of my unborn child. I was a prostitute. I was an adulteress, more times than I can count. I tried to kill my sister. I was a thief and a liar. I had ravaged my body with drugs. I didn't protect my children. I didn't protect them from having to watch men repeatedly abuse their mother. I didn't protect my children from having to watch me make horrendous choices. They had a front row seat to each bitter divorce. They were hurt by all of it. My soul was enslaved to the devil's lies, and they paid the price.

Yet in all the times of deep darkness, there was a Light that never deserted me. Then God spoke. He spoke to me through His **Word**. "Willie, I began the good work within you, and I will continue to work in your life until I am finally finished on the day when I return."[23] I remembered reading that passage from the Bible as a new Christian many years prior to all this. The Lord was faithful to bring it back to my remembrance when I needed it the most. He pierced my heart with this truth. God's Word is alive!

By the unbelievable grace and mercy of God alone, my children are incredible human beings. Do they have scars and painful memories? Yes. But they are laying it all at the feet of a Sovereign Savior.

After the crash in 2010, the corporation went belly up and the Europeans took their technology and went back home. I remained in Oklahoma, but I was no longer employed. I struggled to support myself. My pastor, Pastor Bob and his wife Pat, invited me to live with them while I was still trying to pick up all the pieces Charles had left behind. They genuinely loved me and spoke life over me. They corrected me in love and gave me the courage to endure the season. I will forever be grateful for all their kindness toward me.

Although Charles had said all our companies were "in the black," that my medical bills had been paid, and that our insurance policies were in place, those turned out to be all lies. I was bankrupt. He had even told me there were separate accounts for my children, each with approximately fifty thousand in them. There were no such accounts. I was left with substantial debt.

He often had me borrow money from my bank or credit unions, because at the time my credit was impeccable. He said we needed it to invest in our businesses. The money was never invested into the businesses. Instead, he would buy a new boat, motorcycle, or car. I believed his lies. Charles claimed the money to buy all the luxuries came from day trading. I didn't question him. More lies!

As I said before, the repercussions of challenging him were not worth it. It is hard to explain the control he had over my mind. It was demonic. I know that now.

Friend, if you are struggling through life with shackles you cannot break free from, or in a volatile (physical, emotional, or psychological) relationship or marriage, please seek legitimate Christian counseling. You can also reach out to your local church or open up to someone you know you can trust.

You can find my email at the end of this letter. Be sure to contact me so I can forward your situation to our prayer team. God loves you and has a plan for your life. It's a good plan, and you can trust Him to accomplish it.

14

Moving Forward

Unable to fully support myself yet, and still reeling from all that had transpired in my life, my dear friends, Sis and her husband Rod, asked me to come stay with them for a while. They knew I still needed a safe place to heal, but I also needed to be closer to my job. Sis had been through trauma of her own and had sought counseling to get through it. I knew I could trust her with the truth of who Charles really was. They both loved me deeply and continually spoke Truth and Light into my life. I will never be able to articulate how immensely grateful I am for the love and support of all those who tenderly and faithfully cared for this widow.

By this point, I honestly believed I was fine. I needed to believe I was done dealing with my past. My mind was tired, and denial was easier than facing anything more. The most recent source of my humiliation and low self-worth was no longer a factor. Charles and his treacherous demands had ended. I could go to my grave with the overabundance of secrets and lies that my soul carried, and no one would be the wiser. This was insanity because nothing in my soul was fixed. Just hidden.

I loved my job as a personal medical assistant to a precious little boy. I purposefully chose to ignore all the details of the past seven years. This commitment to live in denial only damaged my relationships with my children even more. I never realized how wounded they were and what the cost of healing would be. My daughter and son-in-law demanded that I seek counseling.

They loved me, and I knew that, but they told me if I did not get help, they would not allow me to be around them or any children they had. Of course, I didn't blame them. They could not trust me. My daughter had every right to be fearful. I was not there for her when she needed me. Charles had used the same gaslighting technique on her and I didn't stop it. I didn't know how. I was so angry with myself. Shouldn't my love for her have been strong enough to keep him from violating her? My daughter and son-in-law knew I was still deep in the clutches of the one who wanted me to keep those secrets buried. Even in death, Charles was in control and I was grasping for any stable straw I could find. I was so completely messed up in my head that the thought of being exposed was terrifying!

But I could not bear the thought of not seeing my future grandchildren and not being a part of my children's lives. Sis, my best friend, suggested I see the therapist she had seen after her divorce. Hesitant, I called and made the appointment. It was a God-ordained meeting. After hearing a little of my story, this loving Christian therapist decided to invest in my life. She helped me peel back the layers of abuse that had made me so utterly fearful of life, untrusting of people, self-abasing, self-destructing, unstable, shamed, guilt-ridden, and completely unable to see the truth of who I was in Christ. Bottom line, I was a real mess! Even though from the outside, I was something quite different. I could fake confidence well. I had years to learn how to conceal what was really going on.

When I started therapy, I was not prepared for the deep pain I would experience, nor was I prepared for the agony my children (especially my daughter) would go through. What evil transpired at the hands of a madman, came out during one of the sessions with my therapist. At that time, I didn't think any of us would recover from it. Charles, by way of "gaslighting," abused my daughter in a way that bore devastating consequences. He exploited and violated her, wounding her tender soul, and I didn't protect her from him. I wanted to end my relationship with him then and there, but I felt helpless under his control and manipulation. After that incident, Charles was bent on keeping us apart. And he was successful for many years. Years I wish with all my heart and soul I could have back. I will always bear a heavy, heavy heart regarding that time. That was my baby girl! Once I understood the truth, I was soul sick for a long time.

For months I sobbed, whimpered, screamed, and literally vomited out of shear agony. I had never in my life experienced so much heart pain. The seven years of my life as a victim of gaslighting was being peeled back layer by layer. **Taking control back from the enemy proved to be the fight of my life**. Harder, even than battling cancer. Harder, even than a childhood wrought with physical and emotional torment.

Yes, I had been hurt in ways that no words can adequately describe. But I was not the only victim. I had to take responsibility for the damage I had caused.

To this day, Satan would like nothing more than to keep me wallowing in self-pity for all the dreadful choices I made over the years. He never stops trying to condemn me with those lies. Of course, I wish there were supernatural do-overs. But instead, we work out our own salvation with fear and trembling, by the power of the Holy Spirit.[24] In doing so, we are **storming the gates of hell!** We are fighting against the spiritual forces of evil—literally![25] It takes effort and prayer and a total relinquishing of our lives to the One who gave us life. This is not for the fainthearted, but it is eternally worth it. And we are not alone in this fight. The Holy Spirit is there with us every step of the way!

There was a lot of healing that needed to be done, and my sweet Jesus met me there in that very dear counselor's home. I began a journey of reconciliation that started from my earliest memory at age ten and continued to the present.

Satan wasn't finished with me yet, but neither was God! I was reminded continually that greater is He that is in me, than he that is in the world![26] He also promised to never leave me or forsake me.[27] How I counted on that. The Lord was always faithful to show Himself to me in so many beautiful ways so that I would not get discouraged. Satan was angry, and he was going to use whatever means he could to convince me that my sin was too great for the grace of God to cover and too awful for my children to forgive.

So how do we recover from so much devastation? How do we hope again? We BELIEVE! We believe He is who He says He is, and who He says we are in Him!

I knew already that the battle had already been fought and won by the blood of Jesus at the cross and through His resurrection.[28] I came through everything battered and bruised, but I came through it a conqueror! Not because of anything I had done, but because of who God is! He is love, mercy, forgiveness, grace, and the kindest Father anyone could possibly want. There are no words. There is no adequate description for how deep the love of Jesus goes. It compares to nothing!

I still had to personally take charge of my life. We all do. The Lord walks with us, even when the road is dark and lonely, and even when we are still insecure. But we are still responsible for our own choices. At this point, I was finally making choices that glorified God, because my heart's desire was to please Him and walk in obedience. That is what surrender truly is! It is the only road to liberty and the only bridge to hope, and it can only be accomplished with the help of his Holy Spirit.

For Christians, the goal is to surrender our will and desires to God daily. Although we continue to struggle with the forces of darkness, we can be certain that the victory is ours! It is **in** the battle that we gain strength and learn to overcome.

"For we wrestle not against flesh and blood [humankind], but against principalities, against powers, against the rulers of the darkness of this world, against spiritual wickedness in high places."[29]

I still had to fight! I had to fight like I had never fought before. I fought for my sanity, I fought for my childhood, and I fought to reject the lies forced on me by men and women alike. I fought for the hearts and minds of my own children. I fought for my child, the one unjustly sentenced to death. I fought for what was just and good and pure. I fought the hardest for what was true! True about my Heavenly Father and about me.

Unless we know what is true, it is impossible to be free. It is only in that personal relationship with Jesus, and the power of His Holy Spirit, through the Living Word of God, that freedom exists at all. Knowing Christ and His Word equips us with the weapons to fight with. We must stay saturated in the Word, and the Holy Spirit will show each one of us how to become **more than conquerors!** The God of Heaven's armies will fight for us!

Another important aspect of freedom is in connecting with other believers who we feel safe with. Divulging your own hidden shame and inner secrets is liberating, and it takes the power away from the enemy! Satan has used guilt and shame to keep us shackled to our pasts for way too long. It's time to fight back!

Do you want to be whole? To be healed? Jesus came for those whose souls are sick. He didn't come for those who think they have it all together and think they can do life without Him. Jesus said, "Healthy people don't need a doctor—sick people do. I have come to call not those who think they are righteous, but those who know they are sinners."[30]

My entire life is a testimony of the unmerited favor and matchless grace of God. His mercy is unchanging, and His infinite love toward us is unrivaled.

What can emerge from the ashes of life's firestorms? Hope, confidence, optimism, anticipation, courage, faith, dreams, trust, and love—to name a few. I know for certain the unconditional love Jesus has for me. He changed me from the inside out! During therapy, He opened the floodgates of my heart, and as the dam broke, He was there. Not a single tear was wasted. As every new and painful memory was uncovered, He was there to hold me close to His heart. When it got hard and I wanted to quit, He whispered to my spirit and said, "It will be worth it all, Willie. I promise." He set me free to experience unhindered worship. He put new songs in my heart. Jesus renewed my mind by speaking His Word over every hurt, every failure, and every bit of chaos life threw at me. Nothing is too difficult for our God.

He understood my nature and my propensity for drifting away and forgetting all the many ways He delivered me from harm and death. Yet in His great love for me, even then His grace covered me, healed me, forgave me, and brought me back to the cross—the place of freedom. Freedom to love and forgive myself and to love and forgive others. He repaired my soul (my mind, will, and emotions), and in that miracle of all miracles, He brought healing and fullness of joy to His daughter—me! I spent my whole life feeling dirty and undeserving of any good thing. But now I feel spotless and pure.

The Lord says, "I will give you a new heart and put a new spirit in you; I will remove from you your heart of stone and give you a heart of flesh."[31] I have read and heard this verse many times and thought about how God replaces our blind, stubborn hearts with sensitive, obedient hearts. But as I was finishing this letter to you, the Lord showed me a much deeper meaning.

The heart of stone He is removing is the law of sin and death. The law condemned me, judged me, and sentenced me to hell. But Jesus took on the curse of the law by way of the cross and gave me Himself.[32] His love was poured out for me there, and He left His Spirit as my guarantee to guide and comfort me, to reveal truth to me, and to lead me in the way everlasting! His heart became my heart because Jesus fulfilled the requirements of the law! He paid my sin debt in full! I am a free woman. The blood of the Passover Lamb has been applied to the doorpost of my heart.[33] I am liberated from that awful curse!

Thank You, Jesus! Thank You so much! Through it all, the Lord gave back to me everything that was lost or stolen, including my dad.

15

Nothing Between Us

I know that at this point if I were you reading this letter, I might have a pretty sour stomach towards Willie's dad. But please understand. Jesus is the Redeemer. He came to save, to restore, and to make new. Whether God intervenes early on in a life or if He waits until the end, that is His divine prerogative.

Ever since the time at the farm, the way my dad tenderly put Porky back together, I could only imagine experiencing something as wonderful as **love** between me and my dad. When I became a Christian, it became a deep desire to not only love and be loved by him but to see him saved. I knew God meant for me to be the one to share the Gospel with him. I also knew the power of intimidation he still had over me. The fear of rejection was a strong deterrent. But if I let that fear and rejection take the place of trusting Jesus to work it out, I would have spent the rest of my life mourning over that loss of missed opportunity, and Satan would have surely used it against me.

Now the time had come when time was running short for my dad. I wondered if I would have the courage first, and then the opportunity to experience healing with him before he died. I don't know what I expected to happen. But in my imagination, I saw myself going to him, taking his hand, and praying with him. I imagined telling him that I loved him and forgave him. I prayed I would be the one to lead him to Christ, and he would receive eternal life. As I was driving to my parents, knowing that soon I would come face to face with fear, doubt, anxiety, and even sadness, I prayed one more simple prayer, "Lord, please."

When I arrived, most of the family were gathered at the house. My sister Ann, while tending to Mom, made it possible for Jean to take care of all the other responsibilities. This was where Jean felt most needed, and I know that having control in this moment was helping her cope. So, I simply made myself available to her.

Two days had passed, and Dad was declining rapidly. My heart was getting anxious because Dad's bedroom was never without another family member in it. When would I make my move? I started to wonder if it wasn't meant to be. And if so, why? Just then, Ann came out of my dad's room and walked up to me and stopped. Was she going to tell me that Dad had passed? Inwardly I began to shake. "No Lord, please no!" Instead, she said, "Willie, Dad is asking to see you. He wants to see you *alone.*" I could hardly breathe. Why would he make that request? The trepidation in my heart was beating so loudly, you could have heard it in the next room. (*This was a divine moment. I knew it! God prepared this moment before the foundation of the world.*) I took a deep breath and entered his room.

I knelt by his bed, took his hand, and silently prayed. When I looked up, his eyes were closed, his face sunken and ashen in color. But then he squeezed my hand, and I knew my prayers were being answered in this long-awaited moment. Something was welling up inside my heart, and I knew the Holy Spirit was there and in control every step of the way. He gave me such peace that the words came easily. I squeezed back and told him that I loved him. I told him that I forgave him and held nothing against him. I told him the past was covered in something so much more powerful than our words. The power of the cross was at work here!

Something so beautiful was happening to me in this moment. I knew what I was saying to my dad about our relationship was true. I felt it. It was so tangible that it took me off guard in a miraculous wonderful way!

It was then I asked him to make sure he was right with Jesus. I watched how his spirit struggled with the Spirit of God. I was in awe of what I was experiencing. Suddenly he spoke. As he labored with each word, he voiced his repentance to me as best he knew how. He said, "Willie, I wasn't even thirty and had six kids. You didn't deserve that cruelty." I understood his heart. In that moment, the tears that had been trapped deep in the cistern of my soul for years flowed down my face. All the turmoil surrounding me and my dad instantly fell away. There was a peace in my heart that I cannot explain, only that it surpassed my understanding. It was the peace of Christ. It was the power of forgiveness!

Three times that night my dad told me, "It was time." I knew the battle for him was over and he was victorious.

The following day, he too felt that peace. He slipped into a coma and died. I know I will see him again in glory, and we will have eternity to make up for lost time. Could there be a more befitting ending to this incredible story? I think not!

NOTHING BETWEEN US

All that Matters

Dad, all of life we do our best
Nothing more, and nothing less
Though trials come, love prevails
Because God is Love and He never fails

Those years we lost, may seem unfair
Pain and sorrow are the load we bare, yet
Through broken dreams, our hearts beat as one
By a gracious Father and His merciful Son

All that matters between you and me
Is that we both look forward to Eternity
I love you, Daddy, always have, and always will
No matter what, I love you still

The day will come when our souls will sleep
Nevermore again to weep
And in that moment, those joys we missed
Will be fulfilled with a holy kiss

For all the things we thought were lack
In heaven, they are given back
Then you and I will wander free
I love you, Daddy, can't you see?
All that matters between you and me
Is that we both look forward to Eternity
I love you, Daddy, always have, and always will
No matter what, I love you still

Love, Willie

16

THE POWER OF THE TONGUE

Remember the wonderful woman who cared for my children and led me to the Lord? Cathy believed that the tongue is a doorway of life for our soul. What our tongue produces has eternal implications because it reveals what is in our hearts. So, what we confess out of our mouth is a gamechanger!

For many years I squelched all the wonderful, positive declarations she spoke over me. I never thought myself worthy of those affirmations. I thought the Willie I knew was the Willie I would always be. But Cathy never gave up on me. She said, "Willie, death and life are in the power of the tongue."[34] She said the stakes could not be higher because words can crush the human spirit or save it.

Our words win wars. Personal wars. The wars within. The most important weapon in our arsenal is the **sword of the Spirit**, which is the **Word of God**! If this is true, and I know without a doubt it is, then we can speak to a mountain and it **SHALL** be moved![35] And don't we all have mountains that need to be moved in our lives?

Here, Jesus' words make the point that confessing the Word lays hold of God to **do** the impossible. So where do we start?

We start by renewing our minds. The first step is to choose to do so. Your will is free to choose. *"Set your minds on things that are above, not on earthly things."*[36] We must be careful of what we think and say because it will mold us and shape the environment around us. It can shape even our faith. Our thoughts will rule our words and our words rule our actions, so we must absolutely saturate our minds and hearts with the Word of Truth in Scripture. It is a discipline, but one well worth the effort. It is imperative to our freedom from past hurts, present challenges, and the unknown future!

So many of us find ourselves basing our self-worth on how others perceive us. It could be accomplishments, shame from our past, defining our value based on the way we look, or even setting standards that are unrealistic.

Some of us spend a lifetime trying to convince others that we are good enough. We want them to see us as strong, put together, wise, confident, and secure human beings. Truth is, we don't need to pretend we have it all together. That is exhausting. What is the point of making ourselves look put together on the outside, when our insides are in shambles? It doesn't have to be this way. If only we were able to see ourselves the way God sees us!

We can! We simply need to **believe (by faith)** what our Heavenly Father says, speak what He says, and **He will** move that mountain!

Trust me when I say, I have not come close to living each day thinking, speaking, and walking in these truths. I still have mountains to climb and giants to slay. But each day is a fresh filling of the Spirit's power, and each day is a new beginning. Don't get discouraged when you fall. Just stand up and keep walking one step, one right choice, one act of obedience at a time. The battle is not yours. The battle belongs to the Lord![37]

He will fight for you and with you and beside you all the way!

The Lord reminded me of a scripture. (*I'm personalizing it.*) He said, "Willie, do not despise these small beginnings, because I rejoice to see the work begin."[38] He also said: "The steadfast love of the Lord never ceases; his mercies never come to an end; they are new **every morning**; great is your faithfulness."[39]

So, what is the mountain in your life? What truth do you need to speak over your situation or circumstances?

The Word of Truth that I claim and speak over myself is: "Therefore, if anyone is in Christ, he is **a new creation; the old has gone, the new has come.**"[40]

I don't know what you see when you look into the mirror. Maybe, like I sometimes do, you see all your mistakes looking back at you. Rest assured that if we continue to believe those lies and neglect to **speak the truth** over our lives, Satan will use every opportunity to keep us in servitude. Our only defense is Truth!

Sticks and stones can break my bones, but words will never hurt me. Remember saying that as a child? Most of us said it to mask the pain and rejection we felt when a peer or even a friend called us names or made fun of us. Sadly, for the vulnerable, if we get told often enough and long enough that we are unworthy or that our sin is too repulsive to be forgiven (like once a whore, always a whore), then we will just give up trying. All our efforts to be "good" will simply fall short and leave us feeling even more empty and alone. We completely stop seeing ourselves the way our Heavenly Father sees us. I often wonder if Jesus feels rejected knowing that the apple of His eye, the loves of His life (you and me) struggle with receiving all that He died to give us. But I promise you this. He will **never** give up pursuing us. He will **never** leave us or forsake us![41] Never! Never! Never!

Are you hoping you will finally get it together someday? Are you hoping this next new leaf you turn over will be green and lush and full of life? Maybe you think you can alter this or modify that and somehow make yourself brand-new again.

Well, before you embark on that journey of sheer madness, let me give you some **GREAT NEWS**! You don't have to "clean yourself up" to come to Jesus. You don't have to "do" anything but **believe**! It is by grace you are saved! Through **faith!**

If you **confess** that Jesus Christ is the Son of God who died on your behalf and rose again, and believe it with all your heart, you are a **new creation** right now. Right where you are at this very moment in time! Reach out and take it! It's all yours! It's a free gift wrapped in perfect Love and Mercy!

I know you feel unworthy. I do too! I still struggle with that sometimes. But we have been lavished with incredible grace. God's undeserved favor! We can't earn it, and we certainly don't deserve it. None of us do. But if we will receive this free gift of grace that covers every single mistake we have ever made, grace that covers all our past and drowns it in a sea of forgiveness and forgetfulness, then we are **FREE**! Did you hear that? **We are more than conquerors**! We can begin to think, act, and live like the people we were created to be.

Friends, **OUR MISTAKES DO NOT DEFINE US!** They never will if we belong to Jesus. Our identity is **IN Christ** and in Christ **ALONE!**

Please don't give up. Surround yourself with saints who will **speak** life (the Word of God) over you. Be brave enough and bold enough to **speak** life over yourself.

Keep your feet planted firmly in His love, so you will be able to understand the extravagant dimensions of Christ's love for you. Reach out and experience the breadth! Test the length! Plumb the depths! Rise to the heights! Live full lives, full in the fullness of God. God can do anything, you know—far more than you could ever imagine or guess or request in your wildest dreams![42]

I want you to look in that mirror and proclaim the **TRUTH: "Jesus, You love me completely, and I am**

precious to You. Father, I am of great worth because I am Your daughter and You are my Father." I will walk every day in this truth no matter what circumstances surround me!

Can I share this passage from the Gospel of John that has been meaningful to me through this process? Jesus said, "You haven't seen anything yet, Wille! Before this is over, you are going to see the miraculous...."[43]

Wow! Was that ever true! I have seen the miraculous! I have seen God encompass my life with mercy and forgiveness. I have heard Him say, "It is finished, Willie. You are no longer condemned!" I have felt His warm embrace, and I continue to stand in awe of all that He is doing in my life. Right now, I am so full of hope and joy because He is still doing! Our God has so much more for us! His "doing" never ends. I am so excited for us!

Give yourself that permission to BELIEVE! He will take that mustard seed of faith, plant it in the soil of His own heart, and do for you and in you more than you could ever imagine or dream. And even though your path may be marked by trials and affliction, don't get discouraged, friend. When you feel like that seed of faith you planted is still lying dormant in the ground, remember this: *"For God has caused me to be fruitful in the land of my affliction."*[44] In other words, you do not have to be blooming to be growing, so don't give up.

He also reminds us: "Listen to me, you descendants of Jacob (put your name in here), all the remnant of the people of Israel (in Jesus Christ), you whom I have upheld since your birth, and have carried since you were born. Even to your old age and gray hairs I am he, I am he who will sustain you. I have made you and I will carry you; I will sustain you and I will rescue you."[45]

Isn't that incredible? We literally have nothing to fear. Our lives, beginning to end, are in the hands of our Creator and the One who loves us so much, that He left the glory of Heaven to come save us!

This world may be a challenging place to live in at times, but God, demonstrating His glory through our dependency on Him, is our real story, and He is writing it every minute of every day. We can trust Him to walk it out with us!

I pray I have done an adequate job articulating how good God is and how, no matter what your life looks like now or in the past, Jesus paid for it all. He purchased your freedom! The cost was His life! Never forget that!

May God richly bless you and bring you peace,

Willie

Endnotes

Dedication
1 Jeremiah 29:11

Introduction
2 Ephesians 3:20.
3 Genesis 2:7
4 Psalm 139:13
5 Matthew 10:30, Psalm 139:4
6 Psalm 139:14
7 2 Corinthians 5:27
8 Ephesians 2:8
9 Romans 5:1
10 Romans 8:39
11 John 10:29
12 Proverbs 18:21
13 Hebrews 13:5
14 Romans 8:1 NIV
15 John 8:32 NIV

Chapter 1
16 1 Peter 2:9-10 MSG

Chapter 4
17 2 Corinthians 5:17

Chapter 12
18 Romans 8:28
19 Hebrews 13:2
20 Matthew 18:22

Chapter 13
21 1 Corinthians 13:4-8a NIV
22 John 10:10
23 Philippians 1:6

Chapter 14
24 Philippians 2:12
25 Ephesians 6:12
26 1 John 4:4
27 Deuteronomy 31:6
28 John 16:33, 2 Chronicles 20:17, Romans 8:37-39
29 Ephesians 6:12 KJV
30 Mark 2:17 NLT
31 Ezekiel 36:26 NIV
32 Galatians 3
33 Exodus 12, 1 Corinthians 5:7

Chapter 16
34 Proverbs 18:21 KJV
35 Mark 11:23
36 Colossians 3:2 NIV
37 2 Chronicles 20:15

38 Zechariah 4:10
39 Lamentations 3:22-23 ESV
40 2 Corinthians 5:27 NIV
41 Deuteronomy 31:6
42 Ephesians 3:19-20 MSG
43 John 1:51 MSG
44 Genesis 41:52 KJV
45 Isaiah 46:3-4 NIV

RESOURCE AND INFORMATION PAGE

Gaslighting is a form of psychological manipulation in which a person or a group covertly sows seeds of doubt in a targeted individual or group, making them question their own memory, perception, or judgment, often evoking in them cognitive dissonance and other changes, including low self-esteem. Using denial, misdirection, contradiction, and misinformation, gaslighting involves attempts to destabilize the victim and delegitimize the victim's beliefs. Instances can range from the denial by an abuser that previous abusive incidents occurred, to belittling the victim's emotions and feelings, to the staging of bizarre events by the abuser with the intention of disorienting the victim. (American Sociological Review 2019, Vol. 84)

National Suicide Prevention Lifeline
24-hour hotline
1-800-273-8255

National Human Trafficking Hotline
1-(888) 373-7888
SMS: 233733 (text "HELP" or "INFO")
Website: humantraffickinghotline.org

SAMHA

Helpline: **1-800-622-4357** This is a confidential, free 24-hour-a-day, 365-day-a-year information service, for individuals and family members facing mental and/or substance use disorder. This service provides referrals to local treatment facilities, support groups, and community-based organizations.

National Runaway Switchboard
1-800-621-4000

If you are a teenager and are thinking about running away from home, or if you are already living on the streets, call **NRS.** The switchboard is a toll free, confidential hotline.

LOCAL RESOURCES (Tulsa Oklahoma)

C.O.P.E.S. (Community Outreach Psychiatric Emergency Services)
C.O.P.E.S. is a 24-hour telephone and mobile crisis service that responds around the clock to children and adults experiencing a severe emotional or behavioral disturbance, a psychiatric emergency, and thoughts of suicide.
1-918-744-4800

DVIS (Domestic Violence Intervention Services)
DVIS provides comprehensive intervention and prevention services to families affected by domestic and sexual violence.

John 3:16 Mission
Reclaiming lives, Restoring hope
506 N Cheyenne (918-587-1186)
Bring Christ-centered solutions to Tulsa's homeless.

Oklahoma Coalition Against Domestic Violence & Sexual Assault
Hotline: **1-800-522-7233**
Email: info@ocadvsa.org
Website: www.ocadvsa.org

BOOKS:

From Spiritual Slavery to Spiritual Sonship
by Jack Frost

*The Body Keeps the Score:
Brain, Mind, and Body in the Healing of Trauma*
by Bessel van der Kolk, M.D

*Boundaries: When to Say YES, When to Say NO,
To Take Control of Your Life*
by John Townsend and Henry Cloud

A NOTE FROM THE AUTHOR

Dear friends,

More than likely, you have lots of questions swirling around in your head. I understand that completely. I will try my best to answer them in a timely manner. All you need to do is email me at <u>williekerry58@gmail.com</u>

Since the writing of this letter, I have had the burden "of holding on to my past" eradicated, as if sharing it took the power away from my enemy! Guilt and shame are the devil's playground, and he is a bully!

I do not want us to go another minute letting Satan or his devotees taunt us into believing that we are anything less than a son or daughter of God Almighty. He is King of kings and Lord of lords. There is none besides Him! We are His masterpiece, and His love for us is immense. Believe it, friend!

I have a prayer team standing by, so please let us know how we can intercede for you. The Holy Spirit is with us to help us overcome!

Blessings,

Willie